Unlocking the Scriptures for You

SECOND CORINTHIANS

Knofel Staton

**STANDARD
BIBLE STUDIES**

STANDARD PUBLISHING

Cincinnati, Ohio   11-40108

Unless otherwise noted, all Scripture quotations are from the *Holy Bible: New International Version,* ©1973, 1978, 1984 by the International Bible Society. Used by permission of Zondervan Bible Publishers and the International Bible Society.

Sharing the thoughts of his own heart, the author may express views not entirely consistent with those of the publisher.

Library of Congress Cataloging-in-Publication Data:

Staton, Knofel.
  Second Corinthians.

  (Standard Bible studies)
  1. Bible. N.T. Corinthians, 2nd—Commentaries.
I. Title. II. Series.
BS2675.3.S74 1988   227′.307   88-4495
ISBN 0-87403-168-0

CONTENTS

INTRODUCTION

Paul and the Church of Corinth

The Beginning of the Church

We know more about Paul's relationship with the church of Corinth than his relationship with any other congregation. That information comes to us from the book of Acts and from what Paul says about that relationship in both 1 and 2 Corinthians.

Paul first visited Corinth on what we call his second missionary journey. After a brief stay in Athens, Paul entered Corinth alone. In order to have provisions to live on, he began to work as a tentmaker (Acts 18:1-3). This restricted the amount of time that he could devote to evangelism, leaving only the Sabbath for such work (Acts 18:4). However, when his companions joined him, Paul then devoted his full-time energies toward evangelism (Acts 18:5). At first, he centered his activities within the synagogue, but soon received sharp opposition from the Jews and moved the center of his activities to a house next to the synagogue (Acts 18:6-7). The opposition was so fierce that Paul was evidently beginning to be discouraged about a long stay at Corinth. So God intervened with a message of support for Paul's ministry there, "Do not be afraid; keep on speaking, do not be silent. For I am with you, and no one is going to attack and harm you, because I have many people in this city" (Acts 18:9, 10). Consequently, Paul settled there for eighteen months (Acts 18:11).

The City of Corinth[1]

In many ways, the city of Corinth seems an unlikely place to have started a church. It was a major seaport, an urban area,

---

[1]The information in this section and the two sections that follow is largely a condensation of material included in this author's earlier work, *First Corinthians,* (11-40107, Standard Publishing). Readers who desire more complete information may wish to consult that volume.

a major commercial center, a center of intellectual and philosophical thought, a center for olympic-type athletic games, a center for several pagan cults, a center for sexual immorality, a city in which the citizens prided themselves for their super independence, and a city filled with self-sufficient arrogance. But on the other hand, isn't that the kind of environment that God wants to invade with the good news? Isn't that the kind of place where people need to know that the past can be forgiven, the present can be changed, and the future can be different?

Corinth was located forty miles west and slightly south of Athens on a narrow isthmus between the Adriatic and Agean Seas. It thus became a natural stopover and transfer point between those seas. Consequently, Corinth became a melting pot of various cultures and a major stopover place for sailors traveling all over the world. It was, then, a logical place for Paul's work. Not only was it a place with many prospects to whom he could preach the gospel, but it was also a place from which the gospel could be spread to the world as the traveling sailors and other commercial people were won there and went on their way evangelizing in other places.

The City and the Church

A person doesn't have to read very far in 1 Corinthians to discover that the church was filled with problems. Why was that so? The answer lies in both the nature of the Christians and the nature of the city in which the church was located. All Christians come into the church as babes, and the Christians in Corinth did not grow very fast. Paul spotlighted their problem as a problem of spiritual infancy (1 Corinthians 3).

But another part of the problem rested in the environment of the church. The church will always take on the problems of its immediate environment. And when a church is located in an area where people are coming through from all over the world, that church will also adopt some of the problems of the world at large.

Every problem we find within the Corinthian congregation, we can also locate within the city and its surrounding area. That should not surprise us, for the members of the church came from the citizenship of the city and its surrounding area. Although people come into the church forgiven, every one of us brings something of the baggage of our former lives into the life of the church. That's the way it was then, and that's the way it is today.

The more we grow up into Christ, the more we grow out of our past life-styles. But that takes time.

The city of Corinth was noted for its independent attitude, so it's not unusual that some members brought into the life of the church the problem of "fellowship" (1 Corinthians 1:4). Corinth was noted for its sexual immoralities; so it was not unusual to find some sexual immorality within the church (1 Corinthians 5) and a misunderstanding about sexual relationship within marriage (1 Corinthians 7). Corinth was noted for its famous law courts. Citizens brought into the membership of the church the mentality of suing someone when things didn't go their way. So the church at Corinth had lawsuits among and against its own members (1 Corinthians 6).

Because Corinth was such a cosmopolitan city that was filled with multi-cultures, various kinds of ethical practices began to emerge within the city. Many of them were neutral—that is, not really immoral in God's eyes—but the Corinthian Christians had a tough time determining which ones they could or could not participate in. There were many Corinthians who felt that they should be allowed to express their "freedom" in any kind of ethical practice; so Paul had to address that issue (1 Corinthians 8—10).

Some of the cults that were popular in Corinth had cultic meals as part of their system. Others practiced speaking in ecstatic utterances. Thus, we're not surprised that misunderstandings of the Lord's Supper (1 Corinthians 11) and of the nature and use of speaking in tongues or unknown languages (1 Corinthians 12—14) soon arose within the Corinthian church.

Many pagan philosophers, as well as some Jewish scholars, did not believe in life after death. Some members of the church, therefore, had a tough time accepting the doctrine that there is life after death and that the body would be raised (1 Corinthians 15).

Paul's Ministry With the Corinthian Church

With all of those problems, it would have been tempting to write that church off as a pagan church that had no hope. But Paul did not do that. Paul rightly understood that every church will take on something of the nature of its environment as it is growing up into Christlikeness. Therefore, Paul did not abandon the church, but rather loved it and ministered to it. Nor did his ministry with the Corinthians conclude when he left their city. It remained great and intense.

9

One way Paul continued to minister to them was through *letters*. By the time he wrote 2 Corinthians, he had already written probably three other letters to the church. His first, which they apparently misunderstood, is referred to in 1 Corinthians 5:9-13. Although we do not have a copy of that letter today, we know the general contents of that letter by what Paul said in 1 Corinthians.

While Paul was in Ephesus, members of the household of Chloe shared with Paul some of the problems going on in the church. They probably also hand carried a letter that the church had written to Paul, asking certain questions. Paul then wrote 1 Corinthians in order to deal with the problems reported to him by Chloe's household and to answer the questions in that letter.

Paul apparently wrote a third letter to the church after 1 Corinthians, but before 2 Corinthians. It was written out of deep anguish (2 Corinthians 2:4), and Paul was very anxious about their reception of it. (See below.)

In addition to writing to the church, he also ministered through *visits* by himself and his co-workers. He first sent Timothy to Corinth for ministry with the church (1 Corinthians 4:17; 16:10). Later, Paul evidently received word that things were not going well at Corinth and made a quick trip of his own to Corinth from Ephesus. However, that turned out to be a painful visit for him, probably because the people were so divided that many of them did not receive him well (2 Corinthians 2:1, 2).

After returning to Ephesus from that painful visit, he sent Titus to Corinth (with the third letter mentioned above). He had arranged for Titus to meet him in Troas, where Paul was soon to engage in evangelistic work. But when Paul arrived in Troas, Titus was not yet there. Paul was so concerned about how the Corinthian church received his letter and how they were doing in reaction to it that he left that evangelistic work to travel toward Macedonia in hopes of meeting Titus and learning sooner about the situation (2 Corinthians 2:12, 13).

When Paul met Titus, he received encouraging word that the church had repented and was in positive change. So Paul wrote 2 Corinthians as an appreciation for that report (2 Corinthians 7:6ff).

One of the things we learn from Paul's relationship with the church at Corinth is that no one should give up on the church. Jesus knew that the church would have many flaws when He died for her. The church is referred to as the bride of Christ. Few of us get married without knowing some of the flaws of our mates before getting married. However, our love is tall enough to look over those faults and still see the persons. If someone does not understand that about us, it is because that one has not loved our mates the way we love them. And so it is with Christ and His bride, the church. It seems strange that some of us who are in the church would not love the church as Christ did and remain committed to the church even with its flaws as Paul did. That seems strange, because *we* are the church. To love the church is partly to love ourselves. To remain committed to the church is partly to remain committed to ourselves. For no Christian is an island. No Christian can really grow significantly apart from his relationship with the church. Paul made it clear in another letter that while we are joined to the head, who is Christ, we are held together by every supporting ligament in the body of Christ, the church (Ephesians 4:16). Every Christian needs the church for his nourishment, for his development, for his total well-being.

There are several flaws in every individual family unit. However, every child still needs that family unit—flaws and all—for protection, development, security, and well-being. So it is with the church. So often we are too quick to criticize the church and abandon her when troubles arise. We should learn from the apostle Paul that the church will have problems coming from its environment and from the immaturity of its members, but we should not add to those problems by our reactionary response. Instead, we should serve as ministers of reconciliation amid the local problems of the church (2 Corinthians 5:17).

Paul and Second Corinthians

Paul had been deeply hurt. He had been hurt by his Corinthian brothers and sisters who had criticized him, ridiculed him, slammed him, and slandered him.

But Paul was also hurt because of the condition of the church. Outside of Ephesus, Paul had spent more time in Corinth than any other church we know of. But the church seemed to be weak in manifesting the fruit of the Spirit and growing toward Christlikeness. Paul's last communication to the church was a letter that he wrote "out of great distress and anguish of heart, and with many tears" (2 Corinthians 2:4). It did not seem as if anything was working for Paul. There was not much evidence that what he wrote in 1 Corinthians was heeded. A visit he had taken to

Corinth after that letter proved to be extremely painful for him (2 Corinthians 2:1).

After returning to Ephesus from that painful visit, Paul wrote a letter filled with anguish. We do not know what the content of that letter was, but we do know that the apostle Paul was on pins and needles awaiting word of their reaction to that letter. He evidently sent that letter by Titus and arranged to meet Titus in Troas.

When Paul arrived at Troas, and Titus was not there, Paul said that he "had no peace of mind." That tells us something about the Corinthians and his concern about their reaction to his last letter.

However, when Paul did meet Titus in Macedonia, the report of Titus brought great comfort to Paul (2 Corinthians 7:6-7). The Corinthians had gone through repentance. They were changing. They even had great longing for Paul and concern for him. Paul was elated! And so from Macedonia, Paul wrote 2 Corinthians as a positive reaction of gratitude and joy and victory for the Corinthians.

While most of the letter is written with that sense of victory, there were still some problems in Corinth that Titus evidently reported to Paul. Paul addressed those problems in this letter.

Evidently, some people in Corinth still did not understand why Paul changed some of his travel plans and did not come to Corinth as he had previously announced that he would. So Paul had to deal with that in a way that would communicate to the Corinthians that he was not insincere when he made his promise, but rather that God was a part of Paul's changed plans (2 Corinthians 1:12-22).

While most of the members in the Corinthian church were moving out of their immoralities, there still seemed to be some who were maintaining sinful ties with unbelievers. It is not sinful to associate with unbelievers. Christians must do that, as Paul affirms in 1 Corinthians 5:10. But it is another thing to begin to participate in their pagan life-styles. That is sinful, and that is what some of the Corinthians had begun to do. So Paul had to deal with that in 2 Corinthians 6:14—7:1.

Because of the internal problems within the church, the Corinthians had neglected to store up a benevolent fund for Christians who were starving in Judea. Paul had written to them to do that in 1 Corinthians 16:1, but the Corinthians had evidently let that slip. We can surely understand that, for internal fights keep us inward-oriented rather than outward-oriented. They drain energy from our major priorities.

Consequently, Paul wrote a rather long section motivating the Corinthians toward generous giving (2 Corinthians 8, 9).

Although, evidently, most of the Corinthian members had a positive attitude toward Paul, there was a remnant of people who were still obstinate and were wearing their boxing gloves. These were maintaining a combative attitude. They wanted to continue their fussing and fighting. They wanted to compare themselves with others and particularly with the apostle Paul. Those who were expert in speech criticized Paul for being "unskilled" in speech. Some of them criticized Paul's apostleship and set themselves up as false apostles. So Paul dealt with this in chapters 10—13.

Some scholars suggest that chapters 10—13 should not be a part of this epistle. They suggest that Paul wrote it at a different time because the tone seems to be more severe than the first nine chapters. However, there is not one single manuscript that shows these chapters not a part of what we call 2 Corinthians. The reason it has a sharper tone is because of the topic at hand. If Paul's leadership were undermined by these few, and that were allowed to spread, then the church would slip back to the way it had been before. So Paul felt the need to defend his ministry, to criticize the false apostles, and to give the Corinthians final warning.

The Pastor's Heart

This letter gives us a keen insight into a pastor's heart. Paul accepted the providence of God even though things didn't always seem to go right in his life. When pressures came, Paul saw that as an opportunity for him to be strengthened and to be a vessel for comforting others who were going through difficult times (2 Corinthians 1:3-11).

A pastor is to be a man of integrity so that his word is his bond, although circumstances may cause changes in his plans. But a man must be open to God's way in his life (2 Corinthians 1:12-24). A pastor is so concerned for his people that he never lets them out of his heart (chapter 2). A pastor is to be a servant of God's covenant and not of his own self-will. He is to be a person who is open to be changed by the Holy Spirit and is indeed being transformed daily (chapter 3). A pastor is not to use craftiness, to preach himself, or to consider himself self-sufficient, and he is not to lose heart (chapter 4). A pastor is to walk between this world and the next, with his desire to be with the Lord balanced with his commitment to serve people in this world that God created. A pastor is to live out all that is involved in being a new creation and to manifest what it means to be a minister of reconciliation and an ambassador of Christ (chapter 5). A pastor is not to walk away from difficulties but be willing to serve the Lord in whatever circumstances come his way. A pastor is to rejoice when his people are changing into Christlikeness (chapter 7). A pastor is to be a motivator, encouraging people to share their material goods for the benevolence of others (chapters 8, 9). A pastor is not to be caught up in the kind of war that is going on in the world, but rather in capturing people's thoughts to obey Jesus Christ. When the situation dictates it, a pastor is to defend his position against false teachers who are trying to undermine the people's trust in godly leaders (chapters 10—13).

Look at the above again. Is the need for those characteristics restricted just to pastor-leaders? Of course not! What we read through 2 Corinthians is a description of the kind of heart God wants all of His children to have. For all of us are God's ministers. All of us are to be ambassadors of Christ. All of us are to be ministers of reconciliation. All of us are to use our experiences for benefiting others. All of us are to use our material possessions for helping others. All of us are to be people of integrity. All of us are to be changed daily into Christlikeness.

Second Corinthians reminds us that the church can change. The church at Corinth indeed did change. And God expects every church today to be changing constantly. No church should be the same as it was ten years ago. No church should be the same as it was five years ago. Instead of seeing problems in the church today and concluding that there is no hope, we should see the problems and know that with God there is significant hope for transformation.

But not only does 2 Corinthians remind us that a church can change, but it also reminds us that all of us who are members in Christ's body are to be changing constantly. We are to be continually assuming the characteristics that Paul modeled. What he wrote in 1 Corinthians was still pertinent in 2 Corinthians, "Follow my example, as I follow the example of Christ" (1 Corinthians 11:1). Each of us is to become what Paul manifested with a church in difficulty. Until we are open to change as individuals—

change our attitudes, change our values, change our priorities, change our commitments, change our investment of time, change our use of finances, change our critical spirits into encouraging helpful spirits—we have no right to point our finger of blame at any congregation who may not be living up to what we think they should be.

Any church can change. Second Corinthians proves it! And any Christian can change! Paul's pen shows it.

God wants His church to grow in quantity, but growth in quantity comes out of growth in quality. God wants every one of His children to grow in quality. That can happen if you let it. Let it happen! God wants us to be free to be transformed.

Now the Lord is the Spirit, and where the Spirit of the Lord is, there is freedom. And we, who with unveiled faces all reflect the Lord's glory, are being transformed into his likeness with ever-increasing glory, which comes from the Lord, who is the Spirit (2 Corinthians 3:17, 18).

CHAPTER ONE

An Apostle for Others

2 Corinthians 1:1-11

Much of the Corinthian life-style had been dominated by self-centeredness. They were acting like babies (1 Corinthians 3:1). In 1 Corinthians, Paul dealt with many of the specifics that dominated their selfish attitudes and activities.

We will see later on in 2 Corinthians that the church was going through significant changes. Consequently, Paul followed up on those changes by developing two key truths. First, Christian living cannot be divorced from Christian ministry. Second, Christian ministry is always a ministry to and for the benefit of others. Even when Paul changed his travel plans, he did so for the benefit of others. Paul was so other-oriented that when troubles came his way, he understood that those troubles were permitted by God to help equip him to minister to others who also were or would be going through difficulties in their lives.

It is only when we are willing to grow out of self-centeredness that we are open to receive the truth of 2 Corinthians. The Corinthians would not have been ready to receive the beautiful gems of this epistle unless the members conscientiously committed themselves to change. Then they would be ready to understand Paul's motives and ministry. Then they would be ready to get involved in a ministry for others. No wonder Paul was anxious about their reception of the letter.

Every Christian is called into ministry. None of us can hire a minister to do ministry *for* us. On the Day of Judgment, all Christians will be reminded by the Father of the gifts that He has given them and will be asked to give an account of how they used those gifts and abilities in ministry for other people in the name of Jesus. We will not be judged for our sins. That happened on the cross, but we will be judged for the stewardship of our God-given gifts.

Will we be embarrassed when that day comes? When the Father says to us, "I gave you the gift of hospitality. How did you use that gift for My name's sake?" how will we respond? Will we stutter and stammer with embarrassment and reply to Him that we didn't even know that any gifts existed beyond the first century? Will we be able to say, "Yes, Father, I was gifted by You and I took that seriously. Here's how I used what You gave me in service to others for Your name's sake."

In 2 Corinthians, Paul makes it clear that every experience, attitude, action, and reaction should be understood in light of how those can be translated into ministry for others.

Paul's Greeting to the Church (1:1, 2)

While the greetings that open the epistles are usually passed over quite quickly in order to get to the meat of the text, we will spend more than the average amount of time with these two verses because they are filled with significant truths.

The Author and His Relationships

The Corinthians did not have to wait until they got to the end of the letter in order to find out who signed it, as is so often the case today. Following the common practice in that day, Paul began the letter by identifying himself as the author. This Paul is the Saul who persecuted the church. He was a Jewish scholar who had advanced in status and influence in Judaism beyond many of his contemporaries (Galatians 1:14).

While some have suggested that Saul's name was changed to Paul on the road to Damascus when he was converted, that is inaccurate. Paul continued to use the name Saul for several years after his conversion (see Acts 9:17, 22; 11:25, 30; 13:1, 2, 9).

Saul is a Hebrew name. His mother probably named him after King Saul. Paul is a Greek name. Why two names? Because of the ethnic melting pot of the first century, many Jewish mothers gave their sons both Hebrew and Greek names at birth. That is probably what happened with Paul. We read that Saul was also known as Paul (Acts 13:9).

It is interesting to note that Saul used his Hebrew name until he began to do ministry in the part of the world that was mostly populated by Greeks. It was when he started his missionary journeys that he used the name Paul. That would have been a better point of contact between him and the Greeks. It would have helped the Greeks to know that he was not trying to make Jews out of them. That name would also be accepted by the Jews in the Greek-populated world, for most Jews in the Greek-populated world also used their Greek names.

The name *Paul* literally means little. It is possible that his mother named him Paul because he was a small baby. Some writers do describe Paul as a short man.

It is also possible that Saul gave himself the Greek name Paul as a self-imposed symbol of his humbleness. He saw himself as the least of the apostles and the chief of sinners (1 Corinthians 15:9; Ephesians 3:8; 1 Timothy 1:15). But those descriptions should not cause us to feel that Paul had an inferiority complex. Quite the contrary. He saw himself as someone who had been especially called by God. He saw himself as an apostle of Christ Jesus.

Paul's Function

Paul's function was that of an apostle. The word *apostle* is not, first of all, a word of status, but a word of service. It does not stress prestige before it stresses practice. It literally means someone who has been sent forth. The word was a common one in the first century, used to describe someone who served someone else. It was used to describe an ambassador, a delegate, or a messenger. It was even used to describe "things" that served their sender, such as a letter or a naval expedition. A true apostle could never be independent. He was totally dependent upon the person who had authority over him, and who sent him.

Paul made it clear that the one who had sent him was Christ Jesus. He was Paul's superior. As an apostle, everything Paul wrote was really the message of Christ Jesus. Anyone in the first century who would read "apostle of Christ Jesus," would know immediately that whatever Paul wrote was not his own message, but the message of the Lord. Thus, to reject Paul's message was to reject the Lord's message.

The How of the Apostleship

Paul was not a self-designated apostle, as many false apostles were in the first century. He was an apostle "by the will of God." Paul never had apostleship in his dreams. In fact, he made it his goal to undo what the apostles had been doing. But Jesus called Paul. In the Galatian letter, Paul put it this way, "Not sent from men, nor through the agency of man, but through Jesus Christ, and God the Father" (Galatians 1:1, NASB). Paul was called by God and taught by Jesus Christ, "I did not receive it from any man, nor was I taught it; rather, I received it by revelation from Jesus Christ" (Galatians 1:12).

Paul's Partnerships

Paul reveals two relationships in this first verse—his relationship to deity and his relationship to fellow Christians. Paul's relationship to deity is seen in the words "apostle of Christ Jesus." His relationship to fellow Christians is seen in the words "Timothy our brother." Paul did not see himself as being independent from either God or man. He did not elevate himself so high because of status that he did not relate to fellow Christians as brothers and sisters. Timothy was Paul's "son" in the faith (1 Corinthians 4:17). But Paul was the kind of leader that helped unleash the potential in Timothy. Timothy was different from Paul in many ways. He was from a biracial family. He was timid. He was evidently prone toward stomach sickness. He was the kind of person that cities would allow to remain after they had expelled Paul. Paul was not intimidated by that fact. He did not make the differences between himself and Timothy an issue, but rather allowed the differences to broaden the team ministry.

We can learn much from that kind of team attitude today. Too often, staff members in a church criticize each other, are intimidated by one another, and restrict the expression (through ministry) of their differences. As an apostle, Paul could have said "Timothy my servant," but Paul saw him as an equal brother.

The People

The word *church* comes from the Greek word that literally means "called out ones." A common word in the first century, it described an assembly of people who had gathered together for a specific purpose. The word could refer to a community assembly called together by the officials of that community. It could refer to an assembly called together by a philosopher. The assembly was comprised of the people who answered the invitation. So the church is made up of people who answer God's invitation to become reunited to Him through Jesus Christ.

The church is universal—encompassing everyone in the world who is in Christ. Every person in Christ is a member of the same church. It is the church of God. Paul emphasized the fact that every Christian is a member of God's household and is a fellow citizen (Ephesians 2:19). The church is also local—made up of members in a certain geographical area, "in Corinth." Not only did Paul communicate his own relationship with God and man, but he also picked up those two points when he mentioned the church. The church also must maintain two relationships—with God and with brothers and sisters wherever they are and whoever they are. Paul emphasized this when he referred to the church as "the church of God . . . together with all the saints." As an apostle is not to be independent from either God or people, neither is a local congregation to be independent of either God or brothers and sisters in Christ. When a church becomes insensitive to God, it becomes a club. When a church becomes insensitive to other people, it becomes a sect. Too many churches have built up walls that keep them isolated from their brothers and sisters in Christ. They don't just wall other people out, they wall themselves in. They actually wall themselves in as prisoners in their own dungeons. It is a beautiful and freeing experience when Christians climb to the top of their walls of sectarian attitudes and peak over. What will they see? They will see people who indeed understand some Scriptures differently from them. They will see some people who indeed are practicing Christianity in different ways from them. But they will also see brothers and sisters in Christ who love the Lord, who are filled with the Spirit, and who are in harmony with the Father.

Paul's Greeting

While it was common for a person to begin his letter with a greeting such as "grace and peace to you," Paul was not just writing that quickly and without deep significance. Paul was writing this letter as a person who had been deeply hurt by his Corinthian brothers and sisters. However, he did not wish for them what they had been giving to him. "Grace" is a Greek greeting. "Peace" is a Hebrew greeting. But Paul did not put those two together just to say hi to everyone. The "little" man was here a "big" man. Grace is an action word in the Greek language. It refers to God's magnificent beneficial action toward us. It stresses God's faithfulness to His covenant, which has been broken by man. The significance of grace is that it is the kindness shown by a superior who is under no obligation to show it. Elsewhere, Paul talks about "the riches of God's grace that he lavished on us"

(Ephesians 1:7, 8). It is out of God's grace that we have redemption, forgiveness of sins (Ephesians 1:7), salvation (Ephesians 2:8), abilities to minister (1 Corinthians 1:4-7; 3:10), the sacrifice of Jesus (2 Corinthians 8:9), strength to live through difficulties (2 Corinthians 9:8), and a host of other benefits. A summary of grace is this—God's goodness offered to us.

The result of grace is peace, which is the condition of well-being resulting from a harmonious relationship. It is that condition of the normal and proper relationship with another person when there are no estrangements. Peace does not mean that we have no troubles in life. Paul experienced a lot of problems. But peace is the absence of alienation, of resentment, of revenge in the face of those troubles. Peace refers to the state of an untroubled heart in a troubled world, or even an untroubled heart in a troubled body. For our physical bodies can be troubled with disease and aches, but peace does not allow those troubles to offset the security that comes from the grace of God. Peace is often the deepest when life is the darkest.

Peace from God is expressed in four dimensions. (1) We have peace with God. We are reconciled to God. Our sins are forgiven. There is a clean slate. (2) We have peace with our brothers and sisters. We are not to live like aliens; we are not to be competitive. We are not to be faultfinding. (3) We have peace with the world. While life may present us several uncomfortable blows, peace frees us from worry and fear, for we know who is on the throne. (4) We have peace with ourselves. There is an acceptance of ourselves as children of God who are loved by God. This kind of peace indeed passes all understanding (Philippians 4:7), but it does not pass all grace. It is the result of grace. It is the kind of peace that assures us that we are more than conquerors in this world and that nothing can separate us from the love of our God (Romans 8:37-39).

Grace and peace have two sides to them—God's action and man's reaction. God's grace is to affect our gracious attitudes toward others. God wants peace to be lived out in peaceful relations with others.

We Receive in Order to Share (1:3-7)

We see several characteristics of God in 2 Corinthians 1:3.

1. He is praised.
2. He is the Father of Jesus.

3. He is the Father of compassion.

4. He is the God of all comfort.

In this section, we see our relation to both God and man emphasized again. God comforts us so that we may be able to comfort others. The word *compassion* is literally the word *mercy* in the plural. (Note the King James translation.) That shows that God is available to us in all sorts of difficulties we face. Mercy or compassion is the inner concern of God that is always put into outer action for man's good. The word *comfort* is the Greek word that refers to standing alongside someone to support and encourage him. It is an action word.

Not only is God the Father of all compassion and comfort *for* us, but He is also the Father of any compassion and comfort that is *in* us. If there is any compassion in a person, it is because of God. That is one of the ways that we are made in God's image. Regardless of how hardhearted people become, there is always a rise of some degree of compassion and comfort from time to time, depending upon the situation. Sin perverts it, covers it up, and seeks to annihilate it, but redemption frees us to be what we were made to be—people full of compassion and comfort for others in need. In a sense, compassion is the inner disposition, while comfort is the outer display of that disposition.

When we read that God is the Father of compassion in the plural, that means that His compassion is tailor-made to our various needs. He is very personal. Our individual needs call for personal expression of compassion specifically for those needs, and God offers it.

Paul used the noun for *comfort* in 2 Corinthians more than any of his other books. God is not to be called "Father" by us without reason. He acts as Father. He "comforts us in all our troubles." The word *all* covers everything that we face—both the small and the big troubles, the physical, psychological, social, domestic, and financial troubles. You name them. God stands ready. He's not merely a "bystander"; He's our "stand-byer."

But God does not do that just for our benefit only. He loves us, but He also loves the people around us. He comforts us, "so that we can comfort those in any trouble with the comfort we ourselves have received from God." We learn from this that no Christian is to live in isolation from others. What affects one affects all. We should look at every experience that is permitted to come to us from God with this viewpoint: "How can I use this for the benefit of my fellowman?" God's ministry to us does two things: (1) It helps us in our need, and (2) it enables us to minister to the world's needs.

That Christians are not free from trouble is seen clearly in 2 Corinthians 1:5, "For just as the sufferings of Christ flow over into our lives, so also through Christ our comfort overflows." Just what are the sufferings of Christ? There are two aspects involved: (1) the kinds of sufferings that come because we belong to Christ and (2) the kinds of sufferings we face that are like the kinds of sufferings Jesus faced.

There are some kinds of sufferings that come because we are Christians. Some people are kicked out of their families. Others lose their friends. Some are misunderstood. Some are looked down upon. Some are neglected. Some Christians who move into non-Christian environments find it difficult to do business or get jobs. In pagan territories, some are persecuted and killed. Many Christians are presently in prison in Russia.

There are also sufferings we face that are like the kind of sufferings Jesus himself faced—that is, His sacrificial living for others, His giving up of self for the benefit of others, and His willingness to stand for God's truth over and against the traditions of men that brought trouble to His life. His care for the hungry, the lonely, the sick, and the misunderstood, and His decisions to act for the benefit of others was often at the expense of himself.

Christ did not have to suffer alone; neither do we. God will always match suffering with comfort. God will make available His support to us equal to the task we are facing. He stands alongside of us. Remember, that is what the word *comfort* means. The comfort is the presence of God. And this presence is ours in abundance through Christ. Jesus is alive and is living within us via the Holy Spirit.

Paul had learned to look at the positive side of life. He didn't hold his own individual pity party when things didn't go his way. When he was distressed, he understood that it was for the benefit of others. He used it to minister to others. And when he was comforted, he did not hold his own praise party or pat himself on the back as if he deserved it all. He also considered the comfort that came to his life as equipment to use in helping others.

Paul's positive outlook on life is seen in his positive outlook on people, as reflected in 2 Corinthians 1:7, "And our hope for you is firm." With all of the problems that church had and with all the problems they had been giving Paul, it would have been easy for him to have given up hope. But he never did. He believed in people, because he believed that God was able to comfort people in any kind of trouble that they were going through.

We would have a better attitude toward people around us if we had a better attitude toward the circumstances that touch our lives. Instead of seeing those circumstances in various kinds of negative ways, we need to see the negative circumstances as positively equipping us to help others around us. Too often, we respond to such situations with depression, "I must be unworthy since I am going through this," or anger, "I don't deserve this!" or resentment, "People are being unfair towards me," or pessimism, "The world is rotten." None of us likes to go through the negative experiences that will better equip us to minister to others, but that is life. A mother goes through pain in order to have her baby. People go through agony in order to graduate from college in the programs that can help equip them better to serve others. Being disciplined as a child helps equip us to be better parents to our children—and the list goes on. As someone has said, "Without pain, there is no gain." Through difficulties we encounter, we can better understand what someone else is going through. We can better understand their perceptions about the world and about themselves that may be totally misdirected. We can better understand their feelings of frustration and hopelessness. Because we have gone through those difficulties, we know that there is light at the end of the tunnel, and we are able to be a testimony to the truth that God wrote to His people in Isaiah 43 when He said,

> When you pass through the waters,
>   I will be with you;
> and when you pass through the rivers,
>   they will not sweep over you.
> When you walk through the fire,
>   you will not be burned;
> the flames will not set you ablaze. . . .
> Since you are precious and honored in my sight,
>   and because I love you . . . (Isaiah 43:2, 4).

What Paul just wrote was stated in another way by the writer of Proverbs: "As iron sharpens iron, so one man sharpens another" (Proverbs 27:17). Christians must commit themselves to allowing that to happen. Many times people come to the assembly in pain. They are hurting and alienated because they are going through many different kinds of troubles. But instead of using the worship service, the singing, the preaching, and the prayers to bring encouragement, stability, and trust, it is so easy to bring discouragement to the distressed. Too many times, preachers preach sermons Sunday after Sunday that are designed to bring blame, *vengeance,* guilt, and low self-esteem to the hearers. There have been times that I have walked into a worship service feeling great, but by the time the service was over, I was depressed. The preacher made me feel guilty for things that I had not even thought about doing. Let us use the assembling together of God's people to build up one another and not to tear down each other. Let us use the difficulties we are going through in God's university of life so that He can degree us with a practical diploma that will equip us to minister to others in need.

Difficulties Can Redirect Dependency (1:8-11)

Paul and his companions had gone through some difficulties far beyond their ability to endure. Paul knew what it meant to be depressed. The difficulties were of such a nature "that we despaired even of life" (2 Corinthians 1:8). We do not know what the situation was, but evidently the Corinthians knew. They were not uninformed about what the situation was, but they were uninformed about its intensity. While Paul was going through the experiences, he had first doubted that he was going to get out of them alive. Paul used the word *"hardships,"* a word that was used about an overweighted ship or a beast that was carrying a burden that was breaking the beast down. Whatever the situation was, it was a real load on Paul. It was heavy on his shoulders and heavy on his heart.

Paul said, "In our hearts we felt the sentence of death" (2 Corinthians 1:9). The expression *sentence of death* was from a legal term that described an official sentence of death. The words "we felt," which seem to stress feeling, was not in the original text. The text really says, "We ourselves *have had* the sentence of death." Paul may have received an official death sentence that was a legal action. Perhaps it happened after some kind of court procedure. The word *sentence* literally means "answer." The idea is of an investigation where the judge answers the investigation with this sentence of death.

While it may be true that Paul faced a particular situation in Asia where he stood before a judge who actually sentenced him to die, this "sentence of death" may not refer to any such experience like that at all. It is quite likely that Paul was referring instead to a low point in his life—the kind of low points that many of us have indeed gone through. And some who are reading this may be going through it right now.

Paul was in Asia when all the troubles of the church in Corinth were multiplying, and Paul's heart was indeed heavy because of it. He later wrote that he had sorrow, much distress, anguish of heart, and tears and that he daily faced the pressure of his concern for all the churches (2 Corinthians 2:1, 4; 11:28). The Greek word Paul used for "troubles" in 2 Corinthians 1:4 is θλίψις (*thlipsis*). It is the same word that is translated "distressed" in verse 6, and it is the same Greek word Paul used for "distress" in 2 Corinthians 2:4. It is a word that literally means "pressure." It was a word that was used for the crushing of grain. Grain would be put between two rocks and, as the stone turned, the pressure compressed against the grain would crush that grain. That word came to refer to the pressures that people face due to the circumstances of life. While in Asia, Paul was in a pressure cooker. He may not have been in much physical danger, but his spirit was pressured. He felt that he had the troubles of the world on his shoulders. The "hardships" (2 Corinthians 1:8; see above) graphically described how Paul was feeling about the Corinthian situation and the situation of other churches that he was carrying on his shoulders and in his heart. He had tried time and time again to minister to the Corinthian church, and nothing was working. Because of feeling that weight on his shoulders, which he seemingly could not move, he felt like a piece of grain being crushed. There must have been times when he felt like, "Lord, come quickly." There must have been times when he thought, "Lord, if you are not going to come soon, then go ahead and let me die. This pressure is too much for me." So the "sentence of death" may well have been his own self-talk about the pressures he was going through in life. He was ready to give up. He was discouraged. He was disappointed. He may have come to that place in life where he was not ready to go on. He may have reached the brink of burnout.

Then it dawned upon Paul that he was carrying all of that weight upon his shoulders by himself. He may have gone through periods in his life where he did not turn things over to the Lord.

27

The pressures were "far beyond his abilities," but he was depending upon only his abilities, and then he woke up to the reality that instead of looking inward and outward, he must look upward to the God of this world.

Paul may have done what is so easy for us to do. He looked at the situation and stacked it up against what he thought would happen in the weeks, days, and months ahead and could see no light at the end of the tunnel. Whenever we do that, we sin against the Lord. And I have done that so many times in my life. But the Lord tells us not to carry the concerns of tomorrow into today. Tomorrow has enough trouble of its own. The Lord asks us to pray to God for the necessities we need for *today*, "Give us this day, our daily bread."

It is my judgment that the "sentence of death" was Paul's own sentence that he had given to himself, a giving-up sentence. But when he was on his back, he looked up and saw the God of the world, who specializes in a deliverance service. Paul came to realize that God has always delivered His people out of the pressure cooker. That's the nature of God. Nowhere do we see it better than when the children of Israel had started to leave Egypt, but Pharaoh changed his mind. Pharaoh had the advantage of preparation, firepower, commitment, and equipment. God's people looked at all of that and concluded that the odds were stacked up too high against them. Pharaoh had everything in this world on his side. The children of Israel had only one thing—the God of the world. And when everything was stacked up against them, they had only one activity they could do and they did it. They "cried out to the Lord" (Exodus 14:10). And God delivered them.

I know what it means to go through times when it feels as if the total weight of some difficult situation is on my shoulders and I do not see light at the end of the tunnel. When that happens, I start walking around with my shoulders drooped and my confidence fallen. I drag everyone around down with me. Instead of being a leader with vision that lifts up the mightiness of God, I become a whipped puppy who makes people around me think, "Defeat! Defeat!" When that happens to you, then rest assured that it has happened to God's people throughout the pages of God's history. That is probably what Paul was referring to in this section. He knew what it meant to go through the discouragements that you go through. But God brought deliverance. The deliverance God brought to Paul was the news from Titus. As a matter of fact, Paul used the exact words about that news that he used in this section to talk about his problems: "But God, who comforts the downcast, comforted us by the coming of Titus" (2 Corinthians 7:6). It is very clear by that report that Paul was downcast and depressed. And it is also clear that he was comforted. I am convinced that the comfort Paul spoke about in 2 Corinthians 1:3-7 and the difficulties he spoke about in verses 8-11 both refer to the weight that he was carrying on his shoulders about the Corinthians. He could not see how he could do anything further to help, and then God brought comfort by the report that the Corinthians were changing.

Do you ever feel at the end of your rope? Do you ever wish that the Lord would come again in order to ease the burdens that you are facing, or that you would just go ahead and die and go to Heaven? Then know ye this. God has more rope—not for the purpose of hanging you, but for the purpose of rescuing you.

The point that Paul was communicating, however, is that even this grave situation ministered to Paul's life. It caused him to look beyond himself to God, who raises the dead. Regardless of how self-sufficient we think we are, it all flies out the window when death comes knocking at our door.

Is it possible that Paul had begun to rely more on himself than on God and needed this experience to turn his eyes outward and upward? That certainly happens to us many times. Maturity does not come easily for us, and it didn't for Paul. He also had to battle with weaknesses and temptations. He also went through times when he thought about giving up. Maturity does not come easily. It comes through endurance.

Not only did Paul's difficulty cause him to look to the God who would help him in that present situation, but also to depend upon God for whatever situation Paul would face in the future. Notice the end of 2 Corinthians 1:10: "And he will deliver us. On him we have set our hope that he will continue to deliver us." Paul's interdependence is seen in the fact that he not only looked to God for help, but also to his fellow brothers and sisters. He went on to say that God would "continue to deliver us *as you help us* by your prayers." Paul had a role in being delivered through difficulties—trust. God had a role—deliverance. But Christian brothers and sisters also have a role—prayer.

There are many benefits that came because of Paul's difficulties. It caused him to look up to God in trust. It caused other

Christians to look up to God in prayer, and it caused many to look up to God with gratitude when those prayers were answered. Paul experienced deliverance. His brothers and sisters experienced answered prayer, and God experienced gratitude.

What a beautiful illustration of the community that exists between God and His people is seen in verses 3-11! God knows what is going on in our lives and brings to our discomforts His comfort. But as He does so, He equips us to pass on His kind of comfort to others going through difficulty. When difficulties come, they cause us to depend upon God and also to depend on the prayers of God's people. While some people use difficulties as a reason for leaving the church, we see in this section a reason to remain in the church. The church is the community in which people with difficulties can indeed be helped. That is because the church is a family whose Father is God. And God fills the church with himself.

Do you know what children do when they are playing and get hurt? They run home for the comfort that their parents bring them. And that's what God's children are to do. How do parents learn the kind of comfort small hurting children need? The parents have learned it because they too have gone through hurts and disappointments. Not only have the parents gone through those hurts, but they have been comforted by their parents as well as others. So parents pass on what they themselves have received.

That's the way it is to be in God's family. When we are prone to become too harsh on somebody going through difficulties, let us not forget that we are family. Jesus put it this way, "In everything, do to others what you would have them do to you, for this sums up the Law and the Prophets" (Matthew 7:12). Notice He said in *everything*. We are not to be selective. And notice that He did not say to do to others what you think they might do to you. He said do to others what you *want* them to do to you. The issue is not whether or not they would do it. Many of the people around us will not minister to us with their comfort. But that does not mean we are to withhold our encouragement, our partnership, our companionship, or our support from them.

God ministers to us with comfort. And there is a lot of difference between God's holiness and our unholiness. God does that for us, and there is a lot of difference between His maturity and our immaturity. God does that for us, and there is a lot of difference between His sinlessness and our need for forgiveness. But that gap between God and us does not prevent God from pouring

His grace and comfort upon us. And so the difference we have between ourselves and others should not prevent us from offering ourselves to them in service. That is part of what a Christian community is all about. And that is part of what God has called us to be and to do.

Summary

Here are some practical truths to understand and apply from the preceding eleven verses:

1. A word from an apostle is a word from Jesus.

2. We are to be related both to God and to our fellowman.

3. We are to desire for our fellowman the finest from God—His grace—which results in man's proper relationship to God and his fellowman—peace.

4. Christians will have difficulties, but they can better us rather than embitter us.

5. We are to reach out and touch others the way God has reached in and touched us in the midst of our situations.

6. Power is being supplied to us as we are going through problems. Both the difficulties—"troubles"—and the delights—"comfort"—are to help equip us to make a difference in another person's life.

7. When difficulties get so severe that we know we cannot make it on our own strength, we can be driven back to God.

8. As flowers need rain, so Christians need the moisture of problems to cultivate them for greater growth. The Arabs had a proverb, "All sunshine makes a desert."

9. The danger of having everything always go well is that it can lead us into dependency upon self and not upon God. It can help us think that we are self-sufficient to handle life without God.

10. Our trust in God does not rest upon just feeling, but it rests upon what we know God has done for us. Because we know God has been for us in the past, we know He will continue to be for us in the future.

11. As the apostle Paul was not ashamed to admit that it was God who delivered him out of his problems, then Christians need to be more open to give God credit for what He is doing in their lives. We need to move out of the embarrassment of openly talking about what the Lord has done, is doing, and what we know He will continue to do for us.

12. God answers the prayers of His saints.

13. The apostle Paul in his greatness was not ashamed to ask for the prayers of the Corinthians. Remember, the Corinthians were problem-filled, carnal, and immature. But still the apostle Paul wanted their prayers, needed their prayers, and was confident that God delivered him out of his difficulties partly in answer to their prayers. We all need to be more involved in intercessory prayer for one another.

14. It is impossible for the circumstances around us to strip us of everything we own so that we have nothing to share with someone in need. Our money can go, our property can go, our investments can go, and our family can go, but we still have something tremendously valuable to share with a person in the pits. We have our prayers to give to God on the behalf of our brothers and sisters in distress.

In summary, the preceding eleven verses are saying three primary things:

1. Let's be open to what God can provide for us.

2. Let's be open to how circumstances can better equip us.

3. Let's be open to using what God supplies to us and using what the circumstance equips us with in making a difference in the lives of people around us and do it for God's name's sake.

CHAPTER TWO

Being Both Flexible and Inflexible for Others

2 Corinthians 1:12—2:13

Paul had to do something that he was extremely uncomfortable in doing. He began a defense about his personal ministry. It is usually not wise to spend much time defending ourselves. But there is a time when that is necessary.

When does that time come? It comes when such a defense will benefit others rather than just self. It comes at a time when such a defense will help the hearers to accept the message that we are preaching. When the messenger is not trusted, then the message he speaks will not be heard.

Evidently between the writing of 1 Corinthians and the writing of this letter, Paul knew that opposition had sharpened against him. Charges of "peddling the word of God" and insincerity had been hurled at him (2 Corinthians 2:17). Evidently, some "false apostles" had crept in to challenge the message of Christ by undermining His messenger, Paul (2 Corinthians 11:4).

In 1 Corinthians, Paul had promised that he was going to come to Corinth and spend some time with them (1 Corinthians 16:5-7). But Paul did not make that kind of visit. Instead he made a very short, painful visit.

That change of plans caused some of the Corinthians to charge Paul with being a peddler of the word. In those days, there were many professional philosophers and teachers who traveled from place to place and taught primarily for financial gain. These traveling teachers would gather several students around them and teach until they were able to receive all of the income that they thought they could receive from that location and then move to the next place. These teachers seldom returned to any city, for they were primarily interested in receiving profit from their words. Because Paul traveled from place to place frequently, it was not uncommon that some would see him in that same light. In fact, some of the Corinthians probably said when Paul first left that city, "We will never see that chap again. Once he fleeced us of all the finances he could get, then he left—never to return." Later on in this letter Paul felt the need to remind the Corinthians that he never took income from them (11:7, 8). When Paul did not return to "spend some time with" the Corinthians (1 Corinthians 16:7), many of his critics jumped on that with charges of insincerity, hidden agendas, and making false promises.

So Paul sensed the need to write a bit of self-defense. In this self-defense, he spoke about the need to be both flexible and inflexible in the name of Jesus for the benefit of others. Christians are to be inflexible in their character and in positive thinking, but are to be flexible in plans and even in carrying out promises if the failure to carry out those promises would benefit others.

Being Inflexible in Character (1:12-14)

In our translation, Paul began his defense, "Now this is our boast . . ." (2 Corinthians 1:12). The Greek begins this verse with the word *for* instead of the word *now*. Using the word *for* makes a tight connection between verses 11 and 12. It suggests the reason Paul just said what he did. Paul had just talked about the fact that some of the Corinthians had been praying for him, *for* they knew that Paul's character was filled with sincerity. Because they knew his motives, they continued to pray for him in spite of his critics.

Paul went on to discuss openly his character and motives, which many of the Corinthians were quite aware of. What Paul did in verses 12-14 was to share his inner motives when he made his travel plan (2 Corinthians 1:15). So the character and motives of 2 Corinthians 1:12-14 are tied both to those in Corinth who prayed for him and to his plans. He was showing in a keen way that what he planned was done with sincerity.

When Paul said, "This is our boast," he was not only speaking about the *act* of boasting, but also the cause for boasting. Paul's confidence in his own experiences did not rest upon worldly standards or his own ability. Many times in this letter, he admitted his weakness, but his confidence lay in the Christlike character given to him by the grace of God.

While others questioned his actions (2 Corinthians 1:15-17), Paul knew his attitudes. Those attitudes were given to him by God, and he trusted in them. What he had done had not been done with ulterior motives (2 Corinthians 4:1-5).

Just what was it that captured Paul's confidence? It was the "testimony" of his conscience—"our conscience testifies," he said (2 Corinthians 1:12). Paul did not have a guilty conscience because he had made some changes in his plans.

Apparently there were three areas of Paul's life that had been challenged:

1. His personhood, expressed in his life-style or "conduct." This is seen in 2 Corinthians 1:12.
2. His letters, what he said when he wrote them. This is seen in 2 Corinthians 1:13, 14.
3. His plans and his promises, as discussed in 2 Corinthians 1:15-22.

While some people charged Paul with insincerity, he laid out for the people to examine two characteristics of his life: (a) holiness and (b) sincerity. Neither of those was self-imposed. Paul understood that both of them were "from God." Paul had not tried simply to stir up his own abilities and appear to be holy and appear to be sincere out of "worldly wisdom." He made no attempt to be a good P.R. man. Rather his holiness and sincerity were genuine and were "according to God's grace" (2 Corinthians 1:12).

Holiness deals with Paul's motives. It is from a Greek word that means a person is "set apart to God." Everything Paul did, he did with his commitment to God in mind. He did not do it just to get a following for himself.

Some ancient manuscripts have a different word here. Instead of *holiness* (spelled *hagiotati*), those manuscripts have the word *openness* (*haplotati*). *Openness* deals with single-hearted devotion. It emphasizes the fact that Paul had a singleness of heart. He was not double-hearted, double-minded, or double-tongued. Both *holiness* and *openness* spotlight the fact that Paul did not have ulterior motives.

Paul's relationship with the Corinthians was also characterized by "sincerity." The word *sincerity* literally means "judged by the sun." It is stressing the fact that a person is transparent and upright in his dealings with people. He is not a fake. He is not a showman for showman's sake. It was a word that referred to something being examined for flaws and cracks by the sunlight and through that examination was found to be flawless. When a person would buy a vase, for instance, he would hold it up to the sunlight to see whether it had any flaws in it. Many times a sculptor who had sculpted a piece of art but yet chipped some of it would put wax over what he had chipped and then try to sell it as a perfect piece. But people would examine that sculpture with the sun in order to spot any implanted wax. Paul was saying, "Examine me through and through and you will discover that what I say is what I am." That is so important! For the message will not be believed by people if the messenger can't be trusted. Preaching is "truth through personality."

From what source did Paul receive holiness and sincerity? Paul tells us where the source did not come from. It did not come from "worldly wisdom." Worldly wisdom is wisdom in self-sufficiency. It is rebellious wisdom. It is wisdom that turns its face away from depending on God. Instead, Paul's holiness and sincerity came from God's grace—that is, God's activity in Paul's life.

Not only was Paul's personhood blameless, but also his pen. His personhood, in the way he lived, was characterized by Christlikeness, and his pen, in the way he wrote, was characterized by integrity (2 Corinthians 1:13, 14). Evidently, Paul had been charged with double-talk in his writing. Some had evidently said something like this, "When you read Paul, you have to read between the lines. He says one thing, but he means another." This is a charge of having clandestine motives when he wrote. Paul made it clear that he hid nothing under the table when he wrote. He did not write with a hidden agenda. He made it clear that what he had written, people could clearly read, and what they could clearly read, they could understand clearly. What he said was what he meant, and what he meant was what he said. What Paul wrote did not have even the slightest shade of a different meaning to it.

Some of the Corinthians had read Paul that way, but not all of them had done so. Paul wanted all of them to be able to accept his integrity as some of them had. When Paul said, "As you have understood us *in part* . . ." (2 Corinthians 1:14), he referred to those in Corinth who did accept him without question. That he wanted them to "understand *fully*" refers to Paul's desire that all of the Corinthians come to accept him that way. He wanted them to accept him in his integrity. He wanted those who made false charges because they misunderstood to come to an understanding of him. Instead of having ground upon which to charge Paul, they would have ground upon which to be proud of his attitude and activity.

If we do not trust one another, we cannot build one another up. When Christ returns, we will have a fellowship of unity where we totally accept one another. We are to work for that acceptance of one another and joy in the presence of one another and confidence in the ministry of one another here and now. What we hope will happen when Christ returns is what we ought to be giving ourselves to happening before He returns.

Being Flexible in Making Plans (1:15-17)

Paul had made some plans to visit the Corinthian church, but circumstances had forced a change in those plans. Because of those changes, some of the people were sharply criticizing Paul.

Paul did not understand that criticism. "Because I was confident of this," he wrote, "I planned to visit you . . . " (2 Corinthians 1:15). Paul made his plans being "confident" of what he had just written—that some people in the Corinthian church understood his motives and trusted him. He never dreamed about not being trusted when he made his travel plans and revealed them to the Corinthians. As his letter did not have a double meaning (2 Corinthians 1:14), so his travel plans did not have a double meaning. What he had written to them about his plans, he meant. Paul had previously planned to visit the Corinthians twice—once on the way to Macedonia and once on the way back from Macedonia (2 Corinthians 1:16). However, when he wrote them in 1 Corinthians 16:5, he mentioned only one visit, and by the time he wrote 2 Corinthians, he had not even made that visit in the way he had intended. That would have caused some of his critics to have said that he was just after their finances and not their fellowship. They could have said that Paul had come once instead of twice to get their benevolent offering and then freeload off of them for the whole winter. They would say, "The truth of the matter is that he never intended to come by the first time for fellowship and ministry." They were probably saying, "When Paul writes letters of plans, you've got to read between the lines. He is vacillating. He is a wishy-washy man when it comes to keeping his promises." Paul partially answered that criticism in 2 Corinthians 1:12-14, but he further developed his answer in this section.

Paul was aware that he had changed his travel plans, but it was not because he was vacillating. Every Christian needs to be flexible in making plans. The flexibility needs to have the motives of holiness and sincerity. Their flexibility needs to have as its goal ministry to other people. What is best for other people? Sometimes we make plans that we eventually discover would not be for another person's well-being. And that's the way it was with Paul's plans. Paul did not make his promises with a "yes" and a "no" in the same breath (2 Corinthians 1:17).

What is the application to us? When we make our promises, we need to keep them or give reasons why we do not keep them. People will not trust our word in the sanctuary if they cannot trust our word on the sidewalk. Many times we are very flippant with our promises to people. We may say such things as, "I'm going to have you over for dinner some time," when all the time we are not intending to invite them over at all. We use this approach to stand off from them. But that was not so with Paul. The change in his plans did not come out of a change in his personhood or personality. The change in his chronology did not come out of a change in his character. In fact, the change in his plans was itself made in the attitude of holiness and sincerity. The change was God's doing for the good of the Corinthians. The change was done out of love and concern for them (2 Corinthians 1:23).

We must remember that when we make promises, we should intend to keep them. At the same time, human activities may cause changes precisely because a change is better. We must be more committed to man than to our methods. We must be willing to change our methods for the betterment of people. God can change His plans without changing His purpose or character.

One of the difficulties that many churches have now is that they are inflexible in their plans, methods, and procedures. Rather than being a mark of insincerity to make changes, it can be a mark of insensitivity to fail to make changes when needs call for that. To make plans and then to be so egotistically hardhearted that we are committed to keep those plans—because "we" have made them—regardless of the needs of people with whom we minister is inappropriate. We must continue to be open to God's leading us in a different direction from where our plans had pointed. The Holy Spirit is in us to be our presider, not just our resider.

Being Positive in Thinking (1:18-22)

One of Pharaoh's observations about the people of Israel was, "The Israelites are wandering around the land in confusion" (Exodus 14:3). The New American Standard Bible puts it this way, "They are wandering aimlessly in the land."

It is easy to wander without aim or purpose or positive conviction. But Paul reaffirmed to his readers that his change of plans had nothing to do with aimless wandering. Paul lived by positive possibility thinking, not by negative pessimistic thinking. Paul's message was positive, not ambivalent (2 Corinthians 1:18). His master, Jesus Christ, is positive (2 Corinthians 1:19), and God's promises are positive (2 Corinthians 1:20). Paul tied every promise of the Father to Jesus, the Son. That refers to every promise God has ever made, of any kind and in any age. God's promise of salvation, of the promised land, of sacrifice for sins, of sending a servant, of a new age, of God's universal care, all find their positive fulfillment in Jesus Christ. Literally, the Greek text says, in Him is the "yes" of God's promises. Because we have seen that God fulfilled His promise of sending His Son, Jesus Christ, and allowing Him to die for us, we have confidence that He will fill all other promises that He has made to us because we are now in Christ. So we can now say "Amen" through Jesus. The word *amen* is a word of affirmation about confident trust in the faithfulness and purpose of God. Jesus would put that word in the beginning of some of His sayings that are often translated, "Truly, truly," or the familiar, "Verily, verily," of the King James version. That affirmed the actuality of His Word and action even before He said and did them. It was to identify that which was sure and valid. *Amen* literally means "let it be."

God may have changed some plans, but He has never altered His promises. In fact, sometimes He changed His plans in order to keep His promise to minister to people. And so it is to be with us. Although we can change some plans, as Paul did, we are never to change our primary purpose of serving God and serving the people whom God created.

We can say "Amen" to God's promises in Christ because we know that God is able to keep every promise. He has all power, all knowledge, and all love to keep every promise that He has made.

We should not say "Amen" as an affirmation to our desires, but rather to God's design. Too many times we say "Amen" just because we like something that was said or something that was done, but are we sure God liked it? Our amen ought to carry with it the thought, "Let it be *through* Jesus Christ to the glory of God." If it cannot be done through Jesus Christ to the glory of God, then we should not say "Amen" to it. Would Jesus be involved in whatever we have observed? Would Jesus say whatever we heard? Would Jesus sing the song that we just heard sung? If Jesus would do it to the glory of God, and if we know it fulfills what God himself desires, then we should say "Amen."

The real issue is not just that we *say* "Amen" at the right time, but that we be a living "Amen" all the time. To say "Amen" is really to affirm God's purpose and activity in Christ.

Not only can we be assured that God will keep His promises because of what He has done in Christ, but also for what God has done and is doing in us, His children. Paul picked that up in 2 Corinthians 1:21. God brings people from different backgrounds into a fellowship with each other and with Christ; He "makes both us and you stand firm in Christ." He "anointed us." That means that He has commissioned us to a purpose, on purpose. Prophets, priests, and kings were anointed for service. Jesus was anointed to His ministry at His baptism (see Luke 3:21, 22; 4:18; Acts 10:38). But our anointing is not just a commissioning. It is also an equipping with the power of God in the Holy Spirit. The Holy Spirit equips us to serve.

We can know that God will keep His promise because he has "set his seal of ownership on us" (2 Corinthians 1:22). The expression is a Greek term that was used in the first century to identify the king's insignia. The king would put his insignia on his property, letters, decrees, and other official documents. That seal meant that the property was the king's and that the king would protect that property. That seal also meant that the property was indeed valuable. It was a stamp of identification. The seal served as (1) security—the king would protect it; (2) authenticity and identity—affirming that the property was genuinely the king's, not a forgery or a cheap imitation. Those with the Holy Spirit are indeed God's. In fact, God's own nature (*sperma*) comes in to live inside of us. That's why we are called God's children, because we really are in the Spirit.

Many Christians seem to be uncomfortable with the fact that we have security in Christ. But God is a Father who has stubborn love and hangs on to us in a stubborn way, as any good parent would do. I grew up thinking that every time I sinned, I was outside the family of God, and if I died without repentance, I would go to Hell. But no family treats its children that way, and neither does God, our Father. God's people need to be affirmed that they have more assurance in Christ than many of them have been led to believe.

The fact that we can know God will keep His promise to us is also seen in the fact that the Holy Spirit has been put in our hearts as a deposit, guaranteeing what is to come. When God guarantees something, it is a guarantee! There is no need to weaken it or talk around it.

The word for *deposit* was a word in the first century that stressed two things. First, it was "earnest money"—money that a person used as a down payment on a purchase. That down payment was his pledge that he would indeed go through with the deal. It was also a pledge from the seller who received the earnest money that he would not sell it to anyone else. The word *deposit* could also be translated "first installment." The Holy Spirit is God's first installment of everything He has in store for us. And it is His guarantee that everything He has promised us will come into our lives.

The word *deposit* was also used to describe the ring in a wedding ceremony. That ring symbolizes a marriage, a commitment, a love and faithfulness. That's one reason why the church is called the bride of Christ. God's Holy Spirit is His security deposit to us that backs up God's guarantee of His promises. People need that certainty. We have so suppressed it that insecurity is all about us. People need to become more competent in God and in His Word. God is not wishy-washy, and neither are His promises. And neither is His salvation. When He saves us in Christ, we are saved! When someone asks, "Are you saved?" we should never answer, "I hope so," or, "I think so," or, "I don't know!" When someone says, "How do you know that you are God's?" we should be able to answer, "Because God has given me His Holy Spirit."

The Holy Spirit is the *anointing*. The Holy Spirit is the *sealing*. The Holy Spirit is God's *first installment* guaranteeing what is to come. No wonder Christians sing, "Blessed assurance, Jesus is mine. Oh, what a foretaste of glory divine!" Christians need to live in the power of positive thinking because God is positive, because Jesus is positive, because the Holy Spirit is positive, and because all three of those are the Christian's.

Paul's First Change of Plans (1:23 — 2:4)

After Paul had shown he was not a wishy-washy, vacillating person because he had made some changes in his plans, he then revealed to the Corinthians the motivation for those changed plans.

When Paul said, "I call God as my witness" (2 Corinthians 1:23), he was asking God to condemn him if he was wrong in what he was going to say. In the final analysis, while anyone can see our movements, only God knows our motives. Here is an important lesson for us. We ought to know an individual thoroughly before we condemn his idiosyncrasies. We would love each other better if we only understood each other better. Many of the Corinthians did not understand Paul well; so they criticized him when he made the changes in plans that they did not think he should have made. To help them understand, Paul shared several reasons why he had changed his plans.

First, it was "in order to spare you" (2 Corinthians 1:23). Paul's change of plans was consistent with his attitude of love and concern. It was consistent with his purpose that by his actions people would be saved, not singed. The term *spare you* is a term of a lover with a lover's heart. Augustine once wrote, "As severity is ready to punish the faults which it *may* discover, so charity is reluctant to discover faults which it *must* punish." Love is kind, and Paul was full of kindness.

Second, Paul wanted to come and be a laborer with them, not a lord over them. Paul evidently sensed that the timing of the visit would not permit that. Paul did not come, then, so he would not have to act like a lord over them. We can learn from this attitude. No pastor has a right to lord it over the flock. If an apostle can say he wants to be a laborer with people, then any spiritual leader in the church today ought to be able to say that. Jesus made it clear that His leaders were to really be servants, and not people who exercise dominion over others (Matthew 20:25-28). Even the Greek word *overseer* really means one who looks upon people for the purpose of looking after them. It does not describe one who acts like a secular boss who dictates every movement and has to have every action voted upon by a special board of little folks. The church has only one Lord, and it is time that many human leaders got off their little thrones and quit being lords. It's time we allowed the church to have only one head. The church has one head, but it has many servants. God wants leaders who will be servant-leaders, not lord-leaders.

Finally, Paul changed his plans because he wanted his visit with them to be a pleasant visit, not a painful visit (2 Corinthians 2:1). He had already made a painful visit, and he was grieved because of it. He changed his plans because he did not want another visit like that one. He wanted the visit to be filled with joy. But when fellowship is cut in two, then joy is lessened.

Following that painful visit, Paul wrote them a letter that came out of the distress and anguish of his heart. He wrote that letter so people could better understand him. He wanted them to understand the depth of his love (2 Corinthians 2:4). It was out of the depth of his love that he made his change of plans.

Can't we learn from this loving apostle? Many of the problems in the church today exist because individual members, leaders, and pastors will not budge from their pet ideas and pet projects. Do we really want to spare people? Do we really want to be laborers with people? Do we really want to have a fellowship of pleasure rather than one of pain? Do we really want joy instead of grief? In order to keep our way, we will fight and fuss over such things as the time of the worship service, the order, the type of music, the location of the Lord's Supper, who serves the Lord's Supper, and a hundred other things that bring pain primarily because of attitudes and inflexibility.

The Corinthians' Need to Change Their Plans (2:5-11)

Paul had made it clear that it is not wrong to change plans when the motives behind those changes are correct. Those motives involve God's benefit and grace to other people. Paul then suggested that there were some changes that needed to go on in the Corinthians' own plans and practices. In 1 Corinthians, Paul mentioned an immoral situation in the church that needed strict disciplinary action. That had to do with a man who was living with either his mother or stepmother (1 Corinthians 5:1). The Corinthians were not grieved by that action, but rather seemed to be proud about it (1 Corinthians 5:2). Paul wrote to the Corinthians instructing them to disfellowship that person from their midst (1 Corinthians 5:4-8).

Paul's purpose for the separation was to bring some sense into that man's thinking. It was calculated to bring him to realize that what he was doing was sin so that he would repent from it.

The Corinthians had evidently applied Paul's disciplinary advice, and the activity had done its redemptive work (2 Corinthians 2:6). But the Corinthians did not follow up on the man's repentance with their ministry of reconciliation (2 Corinthians 2:7). That man changed, but the Corinthians did not change. They kept

43

him at a distance and treated him like an outsider after he had repented of his sin. They would not reopen fellowship with him.

The purpose of discipline is not to keep a man down, but rather to pick him up. Although that person had grieved Paul as well as the whole church (2 Corinthians 2:5), that did not give the church a license to continue to grieve him for the rest of his life. For several reasons, then, Paul urged the Corinthians to change and restore fellowship with the man. Here are those reasons:

1. They were to do to that man what God had done for them—forgive and comfort (2 Corinthians 2:7a). That takes us back to the first chapter, verses 3-7. God has indeed comforted us in our troubles in order to equip us to comfort others in their difficulties. That man had been going through difficulties. Discipline was in order, but here forgiveness and comfort were to be the order of the day.

I recently observed an extraordinary act of Christian love in a college chapel. A couple of students who were not married came forward. In front of their student friends, they confessed that they had sinned against God and against each other and that the girl was pregnant. They wept. They owned their sin. They also acknowledged that they did not want to complicate their sin further by having an abortion; so they were going to be pro-life. But they asked their brothers and sisters to forgive them and to help them work through this tough time in their lives. They said, "We don't want to have to go through this alone." When those students finished their confession, their brothers and sisters in that college stood and applauded. Those students did not applaud sin. Those students who stood were not saying, "What you have done is okay." They applauded the couple's courage to confess sin openly and their desire not to complicate it with further sin. They applauded their courage to ask their brothers and sisters to engage in a ministry of reconciliation and help them through this period of time.

People in the church need to experience that from their brothers and sisters. Too many times, we cover up our sins because we know that the members in the church will gossip or criticize or condemn, and will not love as family members ought to love. Too many times, members in the church who hear about someone else's sin are filled with pride and arrogance as if they themselves never sinned. Discipline for the sinner is never done to punish him, but rather to better him. Paul elsewhere wrote:

> Brothers, if someone is caught in a sin, you who are spiritual should restore him gently. But watch yourself, or you also may be tempted. Carry each other's burdens, and in this way you will fulfill the law of Christ. If anyone thinks he is something when he is nothing, he deceives himself. Each one should test his own actions. Then he can take pride in himself, without comparing himself to somebody else, for each one should carry his own load (Galatians 6:1-5).

The church at Corinth that had disciplined this brother was in danger of being filled with too much pride.

2. They were to keep that brother from going into deep despair, "that he will not be overwhelmed by excessive sorrow" (2 Corinthians 2:7). When a Christian sins and comes to own it, he is filled with guilt. That can put him into such a terribly deep pit that he does not see himself as a person with enough value to continue to live. When that happens, the fellowship of the church has failed in one of its most necessary activities—a ministry of reconciliation. Many people who have been forgiven by God have a very tough time forgiving themselves. They must not go through this without their brothers and sisters' expressing and mirroring and demonstrating the kind of fellowship and acceptance and reconciliation that come from God's heart. The church must never be an army that shoots its own wounded or abandons them to die all alone.

3. They were to communicate love (2 Corinthians 2:8). The mark of the Christian is to love one another. Love involves forgiveness. Too many times, a sinner who admits he is wrong is more accepted and loved in a bar than in the church. That must change!

4. The church was to "be obedient in everything" (2 Corinthians 2:9). As the members of that church had submitted themselves to Paul's advice to disfellowship that offender, now Paul wanted them to continue their obedience in forgiving him.

5. They were to demonstrate divine forgiveness. The forgiveness of the Corinthians would mirror the apostle's forgiveness, which would mirror Christ's forgiveness. To forgive is to let go of the sin as if it never happened, and to treat the sinner as innocent. Forgiveness was to be for the benefit not only of the offender, but also for the benefit of the church, "for your sake." If the church cannot be a living demonstration of forgiveness in a community, then why should people in the community want to be a part of that fellowship? If they catch on that the church lives out the

philosophy that "once in sin, always in sin," then who wants to be eternally condemned once they sin after becoming Christian?

6. They were to block Satan's schemes (2 Corinthians 2:11). When Christians will not forgive their brothers and sisters in Christ, then Satan has indeed outwitted us. He has put a fence between Christians. He has brought disunity where Christ died on the cross to bring unity. He causes Christians to bite and devour each other. And when we do that, we destroy one another (Galatians 5:15).

It is Satan who is our enemy, not our brother or sister in Christ who has sinned. That brother or sister is Satan's prisoner of war. If we do not reaffirm our fellowship with him after his repentance, then we leave him to remain a prisoner of Satan. Satan loves it when the church will not take back into its fellowship someone who has sinned. That person is left in the wilderness as a lamb straying from the flock, and no lamb can survive in the wilderness apart from the fellowship, strength, and protection from the flock and from the shepherd.

Every parent knows the value of reaffirming love and acceptance and reconciliation to children who have been disciplined for their wrongs in the family. Such follow-up on discipline is a must for the children's security and development. And such follow-up within the family of God is also a must.

Some Christian leaders seem to think that it is a mark of being wishy-washy if they reach out and embrace with love and acceptance and kindness someone who has been disciplined. But that is not true at all. It is rather a mark of strength. It is imitating the character of God, who specializes in both disciplining us and in forgiving us. Church leaders who refuse to forgive and accept people who have sinned are church leaders who do not walk in the steps of Jesus. They are filled with arrogance, pride, hardheartedness, callousness, bitterness, alienation, separation, and disharmony. If people in other churches or people in the world criticize us for forgiving the offender, then we need to be willing to accept that criticism. The real test of the Christian community is how well we perform a ministry of reconciliation, not how long we maintain a ministry of revenge. Only then can we be described as people who have the peace of God in our hearts and who are called in one body. If Christ is in us, then forgiveness is in us. Paul once wrote,

Christ is all, and is in all.

Therefore, as God's chosen people, holy and dearly loved, clothe yourselves with compassion, kindness, humility, gentleness and patience. Bear with each other and forgive whatever grievances you may have against one another. Forgive as the Lord forgave you. And over all these virtues put on love, which binds them all together in perfect unity.

Let the peace of Christ rule in your hearts, since as members of one body you were called to peace. And be thankful (Colossians 3:11-15).

It is clear in this section that Paul lived his life in total dependency upon the total Godhead—upon God, who is faithful (2 Corinthians 1:18), upon the Son of God, Jesus Christ, in whom all the promises of God are carried out (2 Corinthians 1:19, 20), and upon the Holy Spirit, who is God's seal and guarantee (2 Corinthians 1:22). And Paul surely wanted our lives to be lived with no lesser dependency upon any lesser source than God the Father, God the Son, and God the Holy Spirit.

Paul's Second Change of Plans (2:12, 13)

Paul had already explained that his first change of plans was done out of concern for the Corinthians. Here he explains a second change of plans that was made out of the same concern.

Nowhere do we see Paul's pastor's heart more than in these two verses. Paul had sent Titus to Corinth, probably with the letter that Paul wrote out of "great distress and anguish of heart and with many tears" (2 Corinthians 2:4). Paul had evidently had a ministry planned in Troas and asked Titus to meet him there after Titus finished his ministry at Corinth.

When Paul reached Troas, he found two things: First, "the Lord had opened a door." An open door usually meant that people were open to hear the word of the Lord and be evangelized. That is the dream of every evangelist who comes to preach in a new area. The readiness, openness, and assurance of positive results should bring peace of mind to any evangelist. But it did not for Paul on that occasion because of his second find.

The second thing Paul found was that Titus was not there. Prospects were many, but Titus was absent. So Paul did something that is extremely hard for any evangelist. He said good-bye to people who were eager to hear the gospel. Paul evidently left his team there to do the evangelistic work, but he himself had no peace of mind in not finding Titus there. So Paul began to travel towards Macedonia, keeping his eyes open to everyone along the road, hoping to find Titus. Probably in every village he entered, he asked whether or not a person named Titus had come to spend the night. He was so concerned about his brothers and sisters in Corinth that he just had to know how they were progressing. How had they received his letter? What were they doing with their lives in the Lord and for the Lord? Was his labor in vain, or would the people change? Paul was like a father to them and indeed had a father's heart.

There are several lessons to learn from just these two verses.

(1) Christian workers do not maintain "peace of mind" twenty-four hours a day. Paul later wrote that we should keep our minds on positive things, and that the "God of peace will be with you" (Philippians 4:4-9). It is true that the God of peace will keep us, but it is not true that we always have "peace of mind." Being a Christian worker and giving oneself completely to the Lord does not mean a life full of roses.

(2) Not having a "peace of mind" does not mean that we are not trusting the Lord or that we are living outside His will.

(3) It is not enough to be just concerned about the lost. Paul had an open door for evangelism in Troas, but he left that because there were lambs of God whom he felt may still have been in the wilderness.

(4) God's people must be concerned for their brothers and sisters in Christ. We cannot just bring new babies into the nursery, leave diapers, bottles, and milk there with them and expect them to grow up alone.

(5) Concern for Christians is to extend across the miles and across the continents. We are not to be so independent that we think the problems in one church belong to them alone and do not belong to us. We are linked to one another in a family relationship and in a body-like linkage. Christians in this country need to heighten their concern for brothers and sisters in other countries who are going through difficulties, persecution, imprisonment, and the like. We are also to be concerned about those brothers and sisters in churches who seem to be unwilling to grow into Christ-likeness but are hanging on to the philosophies of this world.

(6) It is also not enough to be concerned with only our brothers and sisters. While Paul had anxiety for the church at Corinth,

he never lost his zeal for evangelism. He could have thrown up his hands and said "It's just not worth it to bring new Christians into it. I have been hurt too many times. I am just going to cease to evangelize and pour myself into those who are already Christians and build quality." Paul was concerned with both quality and quantity. So in the midst of his correspondence and anxiety for the church at Corinth, which was not growing into Christlikeness, he was also concerned for the lost, who did not have Jesus at all. That's why he went to Troas.

While Paul changed some plans, he never changed his purpose and priorities. While Paul changed his chronology, he never changed his commitment. How about us today? What determines our flexibility and inflexibility? What plans are we willing to change in order to minister to people around us? Perhaps one of the marks of Christian maturity is measured by what we are willing to change and for what reasons.

CHAPTER THREE

Victory in Jesus

2 Corinthians 2:14—3:18

The Victory Statement (2:14-17)

Have you ever waited up at night for a teenager to come home—and he didn't come? So you continued to wait, and with every passing minute visualized all sorts of things that might have happened to your teenager? Finally, the telephone rang and your heart leaped with fear. Your hand trembled as you picked up the receiver. Then the voice on the other end said, "Mom (or Dad), I'm okay. There was a wreck on the highway and traffic was backed up and stopped for over an hour. This is the first time I had a chance to call you, but I'm okay." Immediately, you were moved from perplexity to joy!

That's what happened to Paul. We just read that his mind had no peace because of the absence of Titus; so he headed toward Macedonia to meet Titus to discover what was happening in the church at Corinth. As soon as Paul met with Titus, he verbally danced for joy, "But thanks be to God" (2 Corinthians 2:14). Paul then moved from one grand thought to another as he unfolded his praise to God and reviewed how God was working out His victories. However, we have to wait until we get to 2 Corinthians 7:7 before we hear the news that Titus brought to Paul.

Before Paul allowed us to hear the news, he made it clear that Titus was only the bearer of that news. God was the source who made it possible.

Paul's praise began with a word of contrast, "But." Paul contrasted perplexity with peace, disappointments with delight, concern with celebration, trouble with triumph, and a possible defeat with a present victory.

Paul not only said that God "leads us in triumphal procession," but said that God *always* does that. God does not pick us up to

51

drop us; He does not save us to lose us; He does not adopt us to abandon us; and He does not redeem us to sell us out.

Paul pictured the victory in Jesus with a verbal snapshot of something the people of that day had often seen. After a battle, the victorious Roman general would lead a victory parade through the streets. The streets would be lined with incense holders giving the favorite aroma of the general. Behind the general marched his captives. They were on public display as being the general's captives. They were humiliated. They had lost their freedom to be autonomous. They now belonged to another. They were at the disposal of the general's will.

Paul made it clear that the one who caused the victory in the Corinthian situation was Christ. Paul made it clear that he himself was not the reason for the victory, for he was marching behind Christ.

Paul painted three pictures of the relationship of any Christian to Christ:

(1) A Christian is Christ's captive. He leads us in triumphant procession. As Christ's captives, we submit to His will and offer our services to Him.

(2) A Christian is the fragrance of Christ's aroma. While the victorious general would ask for his favorite fragrance to be burned in the incense holders, Christ's favorite is His followers. We are "in Christ" and are to smell like our environment. In a sense, we are living incense burners giving off the fragrance of the knowledge of Him. And that's what this world needs—knowledge of who God is and what He is really like. That knowledge is seen in and through those in whom Christ dwells.

A fragrance either attracts or detracts. Since what we give off is the knowledge of Christ, then that is a message "of death" to those who do not accept. But it is a message of life to those who do accept (John 3:16-20). As the "aroma" can smell either good or bad, so do other symbols of the Christian life. For instance, Christians are called "salt." Salt on meat preserves it, but salt put on a live snail destroys it. Christians are also called light. Light to good eyes brings illumination. Light to bad eyes could bring blindness.

The way we are, what we do and what we say determine how people "smell" us. But whom are they smelling—us or Christ? The way people smell us can bring to them either life or death. That knowledge calls for us to be responsible. So Paul came to

52

grips with that sense of responsibility when he asked the question, "Who is equal to such a task?" (2 Corinthians 2:16).

(3) The Christian is God's spokesman (2 Corinthians 2:17). Christians are not to be spokesmen the way a lot of people are. As we are to be captives of God and as we are to be the aroma of Christ, so we are to be spokesmen of the Word of God with sincerity and truth. The spokesman of the Word of God is contrasted with the peddlers in the world of men.

Peddlers	Spokesmen
For profit to self.	For the benefit of others.
Insincere.	Sincere.
Sent from a human company.	Sent from God.
Thinks he is self-sufficient for his task—arrogant.	Realizes his lack of self-sufficiency and so depends upon God—humble.
The end result justifies the methods used.	The methods must be Christ-like regardless of the results.

What are some ways that we can violate being a captive of God, an aroma of Christ, and a sincere spokesman of God? When do we cease acting like a captive submitted to Him and begin acting as if we are in charge? When do we cease attracting people to the sweetness of Christ and begin repelling them by the stink of a skunk? When do we cease being God's spokesmen and begin peddling our own product?

1. When our heads get bigger than our hearts.

2. When we are more interested in how people receive us than how they receive Jesus.

3. When we make our opinions on any issue more important than God's Word on that issue.

4. When we fail to study God's Word because we have already made up our minds.

5. When we fail to give God credit for working in our lives.

6. When we depend more upon the method we use than upon the content.

7. When we do not allow people the freedom to disagree with our positions, opinions, and traditions.

8. When we do not allow the sweet attitudes of Jesus to shine through us, such as kindness, forgiveness, patience, peace, gentleness, joy, and faithfulness.

9. When we are dishonest in what we claim. (If God told everybody what people say He himself told them, then God is certainly a contradictory God.)

10. When we plan our ministries primarily to get or keep a following for ourselves.

11. When our showmanship takes priority.

12. When we manipulate people to get the responses we want.

13. When "income for our product" becomes a major interest with us.

14. When we are satisfied with giving inferior goods or being involved in an inferior ministry because we know people will accept it.

15. When for gain we misrepresent what we are doing or what God is doing.

16. When we bypass issues that would cut people off from giving or cause people not to accept us.

17. When we tickle the ears of the audience for their amens, applause, or gifts.

18. When we just stick with the topics we know will work.

19. When we are obnoxious with our Christianity.

20. When we try to twist people's arms to get them to accept our positions.

21. When we humiliate people who differ from us.

22. When we purposely steal the sheep (people) from other Christian congregations.

23. When we bad-mouth other workers.

24. When we commend ourselves.

The Credentials of the Victorious Christian (3:1-18)

In 2 Corinthians 3, Paul mentions several characteristics of the victorious Christian: he is transparent before people (verses 1-3). He is confident in God, Christ, and the Spirit (verses 4-6). He properly values the New Covenant (verses 7-11). He is liberated (verses 12-17). He is constantly changing (verse 18).

The Transparency of the Christian (1-3)

The first characteristic of the victorious Christian is his transparency before others. Peddlers in the first century carried with them letters of commendation so that they could get a hearing. We see salesmen doing that today. Have you ever had a salesman come to your house and say "A friend of yours, Mr. or Mrs. _____ , gave me your name and suggested that you would want to see this product." It is not inappropriate for someone to have a letter of commendation. Paul himself wrote a letter of commendation for Phoebe (Romans 16:1). He also commended Timothy (1 Corinthians 16:10; Philippians 2:19-23), Epaphroditus (Philippians 2:25), and John Mark (Colossians 4:10). So Paul was not against such letters for others, but he did not feel the need to have them for himself and particularly for the church of Corinth. He had been transparent before them. His commendation was in his salvation product, not in his sales pitch—in his Immanuel, not in his introduction—in the lives of the people he served, not in letters about himself that he carried.

In a sense, Paul was saying, "My product is you, and that's the letter you must continue to read." It is true that every Christian is a letter from Christ that the rest of the community will read. The community will judge the church by the kind of people the church creates. Paul was saying that his letter was not to be found on paper, but in people. Christians are to be God's mail. The question we need to ask is whether we are first-class mail or junk mail. First-class mail is more expensive and is personable. Junk mail is interested only in seeing people as prospects. Junk mail is interested in profit, not people. Junk mail does not know the people, nor does the sender really care about knowing the people. First-class mail is worth keeping. Junk mail is worth dumping.

People in a community can neglect reading the Bible, but they cannot neglect the message that comes out of Christians who display Christ's characteristics publicly. Christians are to be so transparent that they are willing to be "read by everybody." We need to be sure that people are reading the message that the "Spirit of the living God" has written on the "tablets of human hearts" (2 Corinthians 3:2, 3). That means that we allow fruit of the Spirit to be so displayed in us that people can read what God's Spirit has done in us, to us, and through us.

The Confidence of the Christian (4-6)

The Christian's confidence is never in himself alone, but rather in Christ, in God, and in the Holy Spirit. Paul was quick to give God credit for what was happening in his life and through his life.

Every significant person that God used in the Bible was quick to give God verbal honor. Too often, Christians today shy away from giving God verbal credit. Too many times, we feel that our competence comes from our education, from our personality, from our intelligence, from our common sense, or from our backgrounds—only. But, our competence comes from God. It is He who has made us competent. It is about time that we understood His importance in what is happening in us and through us.

Our competence does not even lie in the fact that we have memorized the Bible, understand Greek and Hebrew, and possess the art of interpretation. Oh no! Our competence comes from the Holy Spirit, who gives us life. Consequently, our competence comes from God, Jesus, and the Holy Spirit. Any other source will eventually lead to incompetence and pride.

The Christian's Value of the New Covenant (7-11)

The Old Covenant would never have brought victory to the Corinthian situation as the New Covenant did. The New Covenant is what God promised in Jesus. The contrasts between the Old and New Covenants are many, including the following:

Old Covenant	New Covenant
Of the letter	Of the Spirit
Kills	Gives life
Written on stone	Written in people
Written with ink	Written with the Holy Spirit
Read by some	Read by all
Stresses externals	Stresses internals
Fades	Endures
Condemns	Makes righteous
Temporary	Eternal
Glorious	Has surpassing glory
Kills hope	Brings hope
Enslaves	Liberates

The Old Covenant was essential and necessary for the New Covenant. The Old Covenant was a ministry of death because it brought to people the realization of sin and let people know that sin condemns. But the Old Covenant could not give people the life to change them and bring salvation. That comes only in Jesus Christ.

The Old Covenant was fading. In fact, it began to fade as soon as it appeared. Its fading nature was not because of its cheapness, but rather because of its temporary nature. The Old faded in *comparison* with the New. In fact, the Old Covenant is absorbed in the New. It is fulfilled in the New. As the outline and dimensions of a beautiful stream are lost as the area floods into a lake, and as the light of a candle fades away when a one-hundred-watt bulb is turned on a few feet away, so the Old Covenant fades with the coming of the New. Paul was not trying to say that the Old Covenant was useless. He was just offsetting the false idea of its permanence, as was being taught by the Judaizers of that day.

The Greek is much more precise in 2 Corinthians 3:11 than the New International translation. The Greek reads this way, "For if that which fades away was *through* glory, much more that which remains is *in* glory." The word *through* stresses a temporary nature. The word *in* stresses a permanent situation. The Old Covenant was passing *through* a stage, but the New Covenant is staying *in* a stage. When something passes through a stage, it is headed towards another stage, and so it was with the Old Covenant. It was reaching out to the New. The New will never pass away. It will never disappear. It will never give way to anything else. We are living in God's last age.

The word *glory* that appears many times in this section is a word that really means character. The glory of God is the character of God. The glory of a covenant is the character of that covenant. The glory of a man is the character of that man. The finest way to glorify God is to characterize Him. The Old Covenant characterized man as sinner. The New Covenant characterizes man as saved, as a saint. No wonder the glory or the character of the New surpasses the Old. No wonder the character of the New will last.

The Liberty of the Victorious Christian (12-17)

The New Covenant brings hope, and that hope brings boldness. Members of the Old Covenant had to cover up the fading temporary nature of this Covenant as Moses did. When Moses was in the presence of God, his face was radiant. But that radiance faded. Moses did not want the Israelite people to see it fading.

That was not because Moses was dishonest, but because Moses knew that the Israelites were easily disheartened and discouraged. Many times they wanted to go back into Egypt over the slightest disappointments.

However, not allowing the Israelite people to see the temporary nature of the Old Covenant backfired. Since they did not see its fading nature, they began to think that the Old Covenant was permanent. Thus, many kept a veil over their minds when Jesus Christ came and were not open to allow the Old Covenant to have its end with the coming of the New.

Surely we can understand that. Many of us are reluctant to change. Many of us want to continue in the religious traditions in which we were reared. Because we are so committed to our past, we become dull—insensitive to truth. We don't want something to which we have given our lives to become obsolete. Many times, it is easier to win a person to the truth of Christ who has never had any relationship to a church than it is to bring a person to a position of fuller truth who has been raised in a church that has whitewashed the gospel.

The Christian becomes liberated from his past. He becomes liberated from the traditions that have enslaved him. He becomes liberated from sin. He becomes liberated from his own ego. "Now the Lord is the Spirit, and where the Spirit of the Lord is, there is freedom" (2 Corinthians 3:17). The Spirit frees us from condemnation. The Spirit frees us from sin. The Spirit frees us from guilt. The Spirit frees us from all the legalistic trappings of the Old Covenant. The Spirit allows us to be flexible, to have different abilities, and to use different methodologies.

There are just a few things in the New Testament that are not open to flexibility, but God gives the Christian freedom in most of their Christian expression. We have freedom with the order of worship services. We have freedom in the time we worship. We have freedom in the way we worship. We have freedom in the way we pray—lifting hands, bowing, keeping our eyes open, or lying prostrate, to name a few. We have freedom to clap in a worship service. We have freedom for a choir to wear robes or not to wear them. Most of what people in a church fuss and fight about are matters in which the Lord has given us freedom, and it is time that we allow other people to enjoy those freedoms.

However, the freedom God has given us is not the freedom to do just anything we please regardless of how it might affect someone else. The liberty God has given to us is the liberty to become what we are created to be—sons and daughters of God, who can grow into Christlikeness.

Freedom is not autonomy. In Christ, we are never autonomous. In fact, we establish many relationships of interdependence. We belong to one another; we live for one another; we are married to one another; we are added to Christ's body and have responsibilities in and for that body; we are members of one another; we are to use our freedom as an opportunity for serving other people in love. "You, my brothers, were called to be free. But do not use your freedom to indulge the sinful nature; rather, serve one another in love" (Galatians 5:13).

To be free is to become unshackled from littleness, to become liberated from ego, to break out of legalistic traditions, and to be set free from sins that have captured us. All of what I have just mentioned prevents us from reaching out to other people with caring and sharing.

Paul has given us here a description of the Holy Spirit, "Now the Lord is the Spirit" (2 Corinthians 3:17). The Holy Spirit is the extended earthly presence of deity. God is always present on planet earth via His Spirit. David understood that when he said, "Do not cast me from your presence or take your Holy Spirit from me" (Psalm 51:11). Again he said, "Where can I go from your Spirit? Where can I flee from your presence?" (Psalms 139:7).

In both of those places the "Spirit" is synonymous with "presence." So to have the Holy Spirit living within us is to have the presence of God living within us, "And in him you too are being built together to become a dwelling in which God lives by his Spirit" (Ephesians 2:22). "And this is how we know that he lives in us: We know it by the Spirit he gave us" (1 John 3:24).

However, the Holy Spirit does not want just to reside in us, but also to preside in us. The Holy Spirit does not want to be just a resident in our lives, but also the president of our lives. To have the Holy Spirit is to have the presence of God in us. To have the presence of God in us is to have the characteristics of God in us.

It is one thing to have the Holy Spirit in us and yet another thing to be filled with the Holy Spirit. We are commanded to be filled with the Holy Spirit (Ephesians 5:18). To be filled with the Holy Spirit means that we have permitted the Holy Spirit's characteristics to dominate our thinking, actions, and reactions. To be filled with wine means that we take on the characteristics of wine. To be filled with the Spirit means that we take on the characteristics of Jesus. And that calls for significant change in each Christian. That is what Paul discussed next.

The Christian in Transition (18)

Christians sing the song, "Just as I am, I come," but no Christian should be committed to staying just as he is. Every Christian is to be in the process of becoming just as Jesus is.

Christians are to be changing daily. And indeed we are! Daily, we change biologically or physically. There is no way we can stop that. Our cells are constantly multiplying and dying. No Christian can stop the biological changes going on inside of him, but at the same time, no Christian should stop the spiritual change that God wants to continue to happen. However, it is easy for many Christians to stifle their spiritual change. Many Christians think like some of the Jews in the first century. Some people believed that all that was necessary was to be a member in the right group. They stressed the externals, but not the internals. Many did not feel a necessity for internal change as long as the right identities were made. Isn't that the way it is for some of us? As long as we are in the right church, have the right ordinances, keep up some of the externals, then why make a determined effort to change on the inside?

God's goal for every Christian is that we become like Christ. Here are some teachings that make that goal clear.

1. "A student is not above his teacher, but everyone who is fully trained will be like his teacher" (Luke 6:40).

2. "For those God foreknew he also predestined to be conformed to the likeness of his Son" (Romans 8:29).

3. We are to "become mature, attaining to the whole measure of the fullness of Christ" (Ephesians 4:13).

4. "We will in all things grow up into him who is the Head, that is, Christ" (Ephesians 4:15).

No Christian is to stay the way he was or the way he is. God wants to transform us daily. The word *transform* comes from the Greek word, *metamorphosis,* which stresses a change that begins on the inside and then is seen on the outside. It describes what happens when a large larvae spins a cocoon and later emerges as a beautiful butterfly soaring graciously in the air. I know of no one who is collecting cocoons because they are so beautiful, but many people collect butterflies. I know of no one who "oohs" and "ahs" when he sees a cocoon. A cocoon is rather repulsive. It is ugly. It seems useless. But a butterfly is a sight to behold. A butterfly repels no one. A butterfly is to the sight what a sweet aroma is to the smell. Christians are to move out of their cocoons that trap them in littleness and move into the beautiful stature of Jesus Christ, who soars graciously in the world. And He does it for others.

When Paul said that we are to be "transformed into his likeness with ever-increasing glory," he was referring to a daily changing into Christ's kind of character. Remember, the word *glory* really means character. We cannot crank up ourselves to do it alone. That transformation comes from the Lord, who lives inside of us via His Spirit. However, we must give the Lord permission to do that. We must be willing to crack open the outer shell of our lives that has kept the character of the Holy Spirit inside and not allowed Him to shine outwardly. We need to release the Holy Spirit to do His work in us and through us. It is like a grain of wheat that falls onto the ground. Unless the outer shell cracks open, the life that is inside that grain cannot emerge to produce the fruit. And so it is with the Christian. Jesus did not say to the *non*-Christian, "Here I am! I stand at the door and knock. If anyone hears my voice and opens the door, I will come in and eat with him, and he with me" (Revelation 3:20). Jesus said this to the Christian. Although Jesus lives in us via His Spirit, He also stands at the door of our hearts and knocks. He wants us to invite Him into the various chambers of our heart for the purpose of filling those chambers with His character.

Everyone of us has many different chambers in our lives. We have a lust chamber. We have a jealousy chamber. We have a temper chamber. We have a greed chamber. We have an ego chamber. We have a materialistic chamber. We have a success-oriented chamber. We have a grudge chamber. We have a tongue chamber. We need daily to open the doors of those chambers to the Holy Spirit. We need to be transparent with Him and openly confess to God what is going on inside of those chambers as we recognize them. What are our thoughts, actions, and reactions? What kind of old furniture do we have inside of those chambers that does not belong? Then we need to invite Jesus to come into those chambers with His new furniture and fill those chambers and make them His living rooms.

We need to take off the blinders from our minds and see Jesus for who He really is. We need to understand Jesus' character in every one of those chambers of our lives, and we can understand His character as we observe Him in Matthew, Mark, Luke, and John. As we observe Him, it is as if we are looking into a mirror. For what we see in Jesus is to be what we can also see in ourselves if we give ourselves to God as Jesus did.

Paul started 2 Corinthians 3 by talking about the transparency of the Christian who is read by all. Part of being like Christ is to be transparent. Jesus was totally truthful with the people who saw Him. He did not wear a mask and try to do a big cover-up, so that people never really got to know Him. Sometimes Christians feel that they need to shelter themselves from other people lest they really get to know them. So they do not admit their mistakes, their hurts, their pains, their problems, or their sins. Being transparent, however, involves our trusting in God's power enough to allow others to see that we are indeed in transition. We play so many games that people who observe us cannot see how God is working in our lives, for we have never let them see our dark side that gets transformed.

We must learn that part of being transformed is to be transparent enough to admit our weaknesses. Then the power of God can and will turn those weaknesses into strengths. Solomon said it this way, "You will never succeed in life if you try to hide your sins. Confess them and give them up; then God will show mercy to you" (Proverbs 28:13, Today's English Version, ©1976, The American Bible Society).

One of the problems of the Pharisees was that they had their outside appearance polished and shining, but had not changed on the inside. Jesus came to work from the inside out, not from the outside in.

The big question is, "Am I being daily transformed into His likeness?" There are signposts that can tell us how well we are doing. For a starter, try the following:

1. Write down all the characteristics you find in Galatians 5:22—6:3.

2. Write down all the characteristics you discover in Ephesians 4:20—6:24.

3. Jot down all the characteristics you find in Colossians 3, 4.

4. Write down all the characteristics you discover in Romans 12—16.

5. Then jot down next to all those characteristics an evaluation of your own life. Are you in nonconformity? Are you in transformation—that is, are you improving in those areas? Are you in total conformity with those kinds of characteristics?

6. Then spend more time reading Matthew, Mark, Luke, and John. Don't read these just to be reading them. Read them to discover what it really means to be like Jesus. Jot down as many of His attitudes, the way He treated people, and His actions and reactions as you can discover. Then evaluate yourself as you look at your potential self in the mirror of Christ.

To see Christ in the Gospels is to see our potential. What a more wonderful world this would be if every Christian were open to being daily more transformed into His potential because the Spirit of God lives in us!

While Christians are stressing eternal life, there are many people who have little interest in eternal life. Who wants to live eternally with all of the mess they are going through now? What many people need to see in the lives of Christians is how Christ affects the here and now. If Christ can make a difference in the here and now, then eternity will have something attractive to offer. So it makes little sense for the Christian to keep stressing eternal life to the non-Christian if the non-Christian does not see a daily transformation that is making life more bearable, more pleasant, more peaceful, more joyful, and more loving in the present. So, "victory in Jesus" is just not receiving good news and rejoicing, but it is also knowing that there is victory in this life for the Christian *now!*

Summary

What are some key truths we have learned from this chapter?

1. God is victorious.

2. God leads His followers in a triumphal procession.

3. Christians make a difference in this world as they line up behind Christ and allow Him to call the shots in their lives.

4. When we do that, we become the aroma that attracts people to the real substance—Jesus Christ! If we do not do this, we become a stink that repels people from the fragrance of Jesus.

5. Christians are to present themselves before mankind without being artificial, insincere, or fake. We are to seek the benefit of others as representatives of Christ, not peddlers of our own product.

6. Christians are to be transparent—allowing others to read them clearly. And as they read us, they can see what Christ is like. But more than that, they can see that we are in the process of being changed into Christlikeness.

7. Christians are to be competent, but not competent in ourselves only, but also in God and in the New Covenant of Jesus Christ.

8. Christians are to live a life of joy because the New Covenant is written in our hearts by the Spirit. It is not fading, is permanent, and has character that will never diminish or die.

9. Christians are to display hope and boldness, and allow people to see the radiance that Christ makes in their lives.

10. Christians are to live in the liberty that the Spirit gives and to allow other people to enjoy that liberty.

11. At the same time, Christians are to recognize their interdependence upon one another and take responsibility for one another.

12. Christians are to be daily transformed into more of the likeness of Christ until people can see us and better understand Him. That is what it means to be lights in the world. That's what it means to be an aroma of Christ. That's what it means to be a letter read by all men.

One of the main reasons that Christians are to meet together is to help each other, encourage each other, and equip each other to become more like Christ.

> From him the whole body, joined and held together by every supporting ligament, grows and builds itself up in love, as each part does its work (Ephesians 4:16).

> Let us not give up meeting together, as some are in the habit of doing, but let us encourage one another—and all the more as you see the Day approaching (Hebrews 10:25).

CHAPTER FOUR

Servant Characteristics

2 Corinthians 4

Courageous (4:1)

Paul began the fourth chapter of 2 Corinthians with the word *therefore,* which connects the previous context with what follows. In this case, it connects the characteristics of the victorious Christian (2 Corinthians 3) to what God had done for Paul (2 Corinthians 4). What God did for Paul, God does for all of His children in order to help us to become servants. God leads us in victory. God makes us competent. God gives us the New Covenant. God gives us liberty. God gives us the Spirit. And God works transformation in our lives.

But in addition to all of that, Paul listed two other things he had received from God. The first is God's mercy, given at the beginning of the new life and continually given throughout one's Christian walk. It was God's mercy that met Paul on the road to Damascus, forgave him, and gave him a new start and a new lease on life. It is also God's mercy that saw him through all the various problems he encountered as he lived for the Lord after that. God's mercy does the same for us: it gives us salvation and continues to use us in spite of our weaknesses and imperfections.

Second (and as a result of the first), Paul also received a ministry. Every Christian is called into ministry at the time he is called into the family of God. God's mercy not only takes away sin, it gives us something—meaningfulness and purpose in living. Every individual needs a purpose beyond himself in order to find fulfillment as a human being. God's mercy gives that to us. Christians are not saved to sit, but saved to serve. We are "God's workmanship, created in Christ Jesus to do good works, which God prepared in advance for us to do" (Ephesians 2:10). Every Christian has been given various abilities according to God's grace, and

God expects us to use those abilities for His name's sake. Many times, the use of our abilities creates difficulties. People misunderstand us. People neglect us. People read wrong motives into what we do. People criticize us. People hurt us. People tempt us to see whether we will cave in to their life-styles. So it is not difficult to "lose heart" (2 Corinthians 4:1).

Losing heart refers to two things, the first of which is giving in to evil. Christians are tempted just as non-Christians. The second idea involved in losing heart is losing courage. In the midst of service, Christians are tempted to throw in the towel—to chicken out. But being a coward is a sub-Christian attitude, for with the coming of the Holy Spirit come power, love, self-discipline, and not timidity (2 Timothy 1:7). Being cowardly is condemned in Scripture: "But the cowardly, the unbelieving, the vile, the murderers, the sexually immoral, those who practice magic arts, the idolators and all liars—their place will be in the fiery lake of burning sulphur. This is the second death" (Revelation 21:8).

There would be no need to consider losing heart unless there were troubles that came for the Christian. So Paul made it clear that he was called not just to serve, but also to suffer. In fact, he made it clear that the reason he was suffering was because he was serving. "And of this gospel I was appointed a herald and an apostle and a teacher. That is why I am suffering as I am" (2 Timothy 1:11, 12).

The current fad that everyone who gives his heart to the Lord will have a life of ease is a teaching not found in the Bible. That is one of those deceptive teachings and distortions of the Word of God that Paul mentions in this passage. All a person needs to do is to look at Jesus and look at the apostles to know that this is a false teaching. That teaching is calculated to get a following for the person who is promoting it, not for Jesus. For if a person caves in to that teaching, thinking that following Christ will bring a life of ease, he will be more likely to quit Jesus when the troubles come. Instead of teaching a life of ease, Jesus taught that His followers must take up their crosses daily. A cross hurts! A cross is the opposite of a life of ease! Paul talked about that cross-kind of living in 2 Corinthians 4:10-12.

Open Integrity (4:2)

Rather than losing heart, Paul promoted losing heartlessness. A heartless person is one who has ulterior motives, one who takes advantage of others for self-gain. A Christian servant gives up that kind of life. Instead, he is filled with integrity, and displays several specific characteristics like the following:

(1) He is up front with others. "We have renounced secret and shameful ways" (2 Corinthians 4:2). A Christian servant does not have hidden motives for what he does. He doesn't take advantage of other people to line his own pockets. He doesn't calculate ahead of time what the audience will applaud, and then speak to that applause. He doesn't plan his ministry for the purpose of the kind of gifts that the ministry might create. He does not claim to be destitute while driving big cars, living in big houses, and flying around in his private jet. He has no hidden agenda underneath his public ministry. Against the word *secret* is the idea of *openness*. The genuine Christian servant has an open door, open books, and an open life.

(2) He is not deceptive. He does not say one thing and mean another. He doesn't believe one thing and say another. He doesn't preach one thing and practice another. He is not an imposter; what people see on the outside is what he is on the inside. The word *deception* really means "baiting a hook." It is easy for a Christian servant, and especially a public speaker, to "bait the hook" just so the audience will bite and get caught on his line. So he puts on as bait exactly what he knows his audience has an appetite for. What the audience does not see is the hook on the inside.

(3) He does not twist the Word of God. One of the most common ways to manifest secret, shameful, and deceptive ways is to distort the Word of God according to the fantasies of the audience. Many peddlers of God's Word know that the Word of God does not say what they claim it says. But they also know that their audience *wants* the Word of God to say what they say it does. They hide, neglect, or twist the real meaning of the Word for their own benefit.

(4) He sets forth the truth plainly. He states it frankly and openly and simply enough for people to understand what the Word says. He sets forth the truth plainly, both with what is said in words and what is lived in actions. By this faithful expression of the truth, Paul recommended himself. This is the same word that he used in 2 Corinthians 3:1. By this way, he appealed to every man's conscience in the hope that integrity would win the day over the imposter.

(5) He is open to public scrutiny. Being filled with integrity means what the Christian servant does, he does both in front of men and in the sight of God. If anyone does not "see" or "hear" the gospel, it is not because the Christian servant has purposely tried to keep the truth away from that person.

The Christian's Content (4:3-5)

If non-Christians did not hear or see the gospel, it is not because Paul had changed it by secret, shameful, deceptive, or distorting ways. It was rather because either the people had not been open to seeing it or "the god of this age . . . blinded [their] minds" so that they could not see it (2 Corinthians 4:4). The "god of this age" refers to the devil. (Compare John 12:31; 14:30; 16:11; Ephesians 2:2.) He is the ultimate source behind any veiling of the gospel.

The devil is in the veiling business. In fact, the main victory the devil wins when he uses people to distort God's Word and to be engaged in wrong motives is that the gospel is veiled. Thus, anyone who veils the gospel through the methods discussed above is really a pawn in the hand of the devil. The devil knows how to disguise himself as a messenger of light (2 Corinthians 11:14).

The results of a veiled gospel are devastating. Here are four results mentioned:

(1) The people who listen to a veiled gospel are perishing.

(2) People who listen to a veiled gospel are blinded. A veiled gospel does not give them the enlightenment for which Paul prayed in Ephesians 1:18, 19: "I pray also that the eyes of your heart may be enlightened in order that you may know the hope to which he has called you, the riches of his glorious inheritance in the saints, and his incomparably great power for us who believe."

(3) The people who hear a veiled gospel are unbelievers. They may be believers of one sort, for they believe the message of the person speaking, but they are unbelievers from God's perspective.

(4) Those who listen to a veiled gospel miss Christ. That is the sadness and tragedy of people's continuing to preach a veiled gospel for their own benefit. They are not allowing people to see "the glory of Christ, who is the image of God" (2 Corinthians 4:4). And anyone who misses Christ is an unbeliever, regardless of how much that person trusts the words of a man.

It is a tragedy that *the god* of this world has caused people to worship the god of *this world*. That is, they worship status, success, money, popularity, and human followings. The glitter of *this world* blinds both leaders and followers from seeing the surpassing splendor of Jesus. It is man's ego that keeps him from seeing God's Immanuel.

What is the answer to this problem? It is not preaching oneself as the person to follow, but Jesus Christ as Lord and ourselves as servants (2 Corinthians 4:5). Anyone who preaches himself has chosen one of the most inferior topics on earth. In fact, he is down to the bottom of his barrel.

Many people conveniently reverse 2 Corinthians 4:5 by preaching themselves as the lords of people and Jesus Christ as the servant of themselves and others. They turn people to themselves and then expect the Lord to serve them and all others by giving them a life of ease, prosperity, and health. But Jesus is Lord, which means that we are to obey Him. A Christian leader is to be a servant. That does not mean people serve us; we serve them.

One of the marks of Christian spirituality and maturity is that a Christian has matured to the place of being a humble servant to others. Jesus said, "Whoever wants to become great among you must be your servant, and whoever wants to be first must be your slave—just as the Son of Man did not come to be served, but to serve, and to give his life as a ransom for many" (Matthew 20:26-28).

Jesus' greatness was seen in the fact that He emptied himself and became obedient and took on the function of a servant. And to that, God calls all of us (Philippians 2:5-11).

It is easy to change the central topic of Christianity from Jesus to some sub-topic. It's easy, but it's not appropriate, even though that sub-topic may be Biblical. For instance, some people talk about the second coming as their main topic. Some people make the millennial issue the main topic. Some people make prophecy their main topic. Some people make baptism their main topic. And on and on the list goes! None of those topics has any value whatsoever apart from Jesus. If a person becomes a walking encyclopedia on any of those topics and has every aspect of those topics down pat, but does not have a personal relationship to the person of Jesus, then he has missed the central core of Christianity. There are many people who have come to have a personal fellowship with Jesus. They know Jesus. They have invited Jesus into their lives. They walk with Jesus. They talk with Jesus. They depend upon Jesus. They relate to Jesus as a person, as a friend, as their Lord. Many of those people may not have all the man-made systems of theology down pat. They may not understand which millennial position is God's. They may not understand how the message of Daniel fits with Revelation. They may not understand all the reasons for and significances of baptism. But they know Jesus and love Him. And those people are having a ball in their Christian lives, and people around them can see a difference. It is those people who give the aroma that draws others to the "glory of Christ Jesus, who is the image of God."

The Equipment for the Christian (4:6)

God's light shines in us so that God's light can shine out of us. But what is that light? Jesus said, "I am the light of the world" (John 9:5).

The light of Jesus is the *life* of Jesus, and that life brings *light* to men (John 1:4). "The light shines in the darkness, but the darkness has not understood it" (John 1:5). That means that Christ's life shines into the darkness of man's soul, and the darkness of man's soul does not overpower the presence of Jesus. Christ's life was living in Paul and lives in every Christian. The "light" is not referring to our intellectual capacities, but to the presence of the living Lord.

Why does He live in us? In this context, Paul spotlighted the fact that Christ lives in us in order to give to us the knowledge of the glory of God in the face of Christ. As Jesus was made in the image of God, every Christian has been recreated to his original image—the image of God. God wants everyone of us to know His character. And we know His character as we observe the face (or life) of Christ. It is Christ in us that makes the difference. He is the equipment that enables us to be used in a way that other people can be drawn to the Father.

Value Inside a Vase (4:7-12)

In 2 Corinthians 4:7, Paul contrasted the powerful with the powerless and the temporary with the permanent. The "jars of clay" is a symbol for the Christian. A jar of clay was a crackable, fragile, and inexpensive vessel. In one sense, Christians are "crackpots." Inside of these fragile vessels is God's greatest treasure. Imagine it! God's diamonds stored in cereal boxes!

Just what is it that is stored inside of us? It is just what Paul discussed in 2 Corinthians 4:6. The character of God with all of

His power, all of His holiness, all of His value has been put inside of us through the presence of Jesus Christ. Why would God do that? Because He loves us? Of course! But in addition, He does it to demonstrate that the power people see through Christians is not there because of who we are, but rather because of who is in us—Jesus!

Paul picked up the theme of the temporary nature of a person's body and the permanent nature of Christ in 2 Corinthians 4:8-12. The only reason Paul did not cave in, quit, or become destroyed, was because the treasure that was in him was powerful, permanent, and victorious. After all, how can you continually hit a fragile clay pot without destroying the clay pot? The only answer is that the content of that clay pot has been in that clay pot so long that the pot has taken on the nature of the content. And that is what Paul shows for the Christian who continues to commit himself to the Lord.

In these verses, we can also see how Paul felt from time to time. He was not immune to difficulties, troubles, or pressures. *Hard pressed* is the term that was used for crushing grain or fruit such as grapes in the first century. (See the comments on θλίψις, above, 1:4, 6.) Grapes are very fragile when the wine press begins its squeeze. Paul had been catching it from every side, but the life was not squeezed out of him. That's because Jesus was the life that was living inside of him. *Perplexed* means to be at wits' end. Have you ever reached the place where you didn't know which way to turn? In a sense, Paul was saying that he did not know which end was up, but that did not upend him. That was because Jesus lived inside of him. *Persecuted* is a word that literally meant to be hunted down and chased like an animal, but Paul was not like an animal on the run by himself. He was never abandoned, for the Christ was living in him. Paul was struck down many times both emotionally, verbally, and socially, but he was never knocked out.

Does the above sound like Christianity is a life of ease and trouble-free skating?

Just what did Paul mean when he said (in 2 Corinthians 4:10), "We always carry around in our body the death of Jesus, so that the life of Jesus may also be revealed in our body"? He was probably referring to the way Jesus always gave himself up for others. Jesus did not just go to the cross after Pilate sentenced Him. Jesus lived on a "cross" all the days of His ministry. What happened on the cross was a visible demonstration of what was happening in His heart daily. On the cross, He made decisions for other people's benefit and not His own. On the cross, He refused to play power games and did not call down legions of angels for His own protection. On the cross, He looked out after others such as His mother. On the cross, He forgave the very people who were purposely hurting Him. On the cross, He identified himself with the riffraff of society by hanging between two thieves. On the cross, He refused to take the easy way out because He knew men needed to be lifted up to the throne of God. On the cross, He refused to defend himself. On the cross, He refused to play the big shot.

That's what it means to die to self. Whenever we are willing to die to self like that, then the life of Jesus is revealed through us. The "death" that is at work in us is the death to selfishness and the "life" that is at work in us is the life of the unselfish presence of Jesus through His Spirit. That touches people! That motivates people! That inspires people! That draws people to the Father! That changes people! And, that can save people!

Behavior Out of Belief (4:13-15)

The Christian is to live his life out of faith. Only then is he not a phony. Out of faith comes our speech (2 Corinthians 4:13). Out of faith comes our hope (2 Corinthians 4:14). Out of faith comes our service for the benefit of others (2 Corinthians 4:15). Out of faith comes confidence (2 Corinthians 4:16a). Out of faith comes strength in the inner man (2 Corinthians 4:16b). Out of faith comes a proper perspective (2 Corinthians 4:17). Out of faith comes the correct priority (2 Corinthians 4:18).

Without faith it is impossible to please God (Hebrews 11:6). When God asks us to act out of faith in Him, He is asking us to do with Him what we do with everything else in life. Faith is the assurance of things hoped for and the conviction of things we do not see (Hebrews 11:1). No person can live five minutes without exercising faith. Faith is really the sixth sense that conditions man's living. A person cannot breathe the next breath of air without exercising confidence in something he hopes for. How do you know there is not something in the air that is going to kill you? A person cannot take a drink of water without faith. How do you know that there is not something in that water that is lethal? A person cannot stop and eat at a restaurant without faith. How do you know that the cooks are not mad at the owners and are dumping poison into the food? A person cannot get out of bed and put his feet onto the floor without faith. How do you know someone hasn't cut a hole in the floor and when you hit it you will just keep going down? There is not one thing that we do in life without exercising faith. Our behavior comes out of our belief systems, and God wants the Christian's behavior also to come out of his belief system in Him and in His Son.

It is out of faith that we speak about God and His Son. It is also out of faith that we look beyond death. Many Christians would like Jesus to come back during their lifetime. Paul certainly would have welcomed that. But Paul also realized that he might die prior to the second coming of Jesus. But that did not bother Paul, for he made it clear that the one who raised Jesus from the dead would also raise him from the dead and would indeed bring together the reunion of all Christians in the presence of Jesus.

It is out of faith that Paul offered himself in service for the benefit of others. When more and more people are brought into a saving relationship with God, then God is glorified by the thanksgiving that those people offer to Him (2 Corinthians 4:15). Paul could say that even though he was going through devastating troubles. In spite of those troubles, he committed himself to be God's servant in the presence of all peoples. And that is what Paul developed in this chapter. He talked about troubles that he had gone through, but he also talked about the service he was going to render for the benefit of all peoples. All of that was true because he had a trust in God, who can do the impossible.

Proper Perspectives and Priorities (4:16-18)

Paul ended this chapter the way he began it, "We do not lose heart." Paul had the right perspective on life. He realized that the outer flesh is temporary and is indeed wasting away. But he also realized that the presence of Jesus renews the inner man day by day. Christians can look worn-out on the outside but be refreshed on the inside. Paul also realized that the troubles we are going through are really little compared to the glory that God will give to every Christian. Those troubles are temporary compared to the permanence of the rewards God has for us. Instead of being outweighed or burdened down by the troubles, Paul just let his perspective about God's glory outweigh those troubles.

Out of that perspective, Paul had the correct priority. He did not put stock on the things that were temporary, but rather on what is eternal. Why invest so much energy on something that is not going to last while neglecting what is going to be permanent? Why commit oneself to the character of the world that may bring pleasure for a while, but will be destroyed when Jesus comes again? Many people devote themselves to the pleasures of uncontrolled sex, uncontrolled leisure, uncontrolled accumulating of things, and uncontrolled ladder-climbing for status. None of that "character" will last. All of that will go to Hell. But what is it that is eternal? It is the character of God, the character of the Holy Spirit, the character of Jesus! That is because God, Jesus, and the Holy Spirit are eternal. The grace of Jesus, the love of God, and the fellowship of the Holy Spirit will last forever and ever and ever. It is unwise to give in to the character of the moment and not live with the character of the Master.

The songwriter has captured this priority of Paul's well:

Turn your eyes upon Jesus.
Look full in His wonderful face.
And the things of earth will grow strangely dim
In the light of His glory and grace.[2]

Summary

This chapter has emphasized some of the marvelous characteristics of God's servant-children. Here are some of them:

1. The Christian has received mercy and ministry. God has called us to both privilege (what He does for us) and purpose (what He wants from us).

2. The Christian servant does not chicken out.

3. The Christian servant renounces ulterior motives.

4. The Christian servant does not bait the hook just to get a following for himself.

5. The Christian servant does not twist the Word of God just to say what he knows his audience wants to hear.

---

6. The Christian servant is publicly transparent before both man and God.

7. Any Christian servant who veils the true content of the gospel is a pawn in the hand of the devil.

8. To veil the gospel by our deception and distortion is to cause people to miss Jesus.

9. Jesus has equipped us with presence of himself, and that is the "light that shines out of darkness."

10. God has put His treasure in our valueless vases, but when He is in us, then we become extremely valuable—not because of who we are, but because of who is in us.

11. The Christian life is not a life free of trouble, but it is a life that has inner strength to live through those difficulties.

12. The Christian life is to be a continual display of Jesus' cross experiences.

13. The Christian's behavior is to come out of his belief.

14. The Christian is to have proper perspective about the temporal and the eternal.

15. The Christian is to give priority to Jesus, who lives forever, and not to gimmicks that are deteriorating.

CHAPTER FIVE

Servant Commitment

2 Corinthians 5

Motivations for Service (5:1-15)

The beginning of 2 Corinthians 5 is connected to the ending of the fourth chapter by a very important Greek word. The word translated "now" in the New International Version is the Greek word *gar,* which introduces a reason why Paul had just finished saying what he said and the way in which he said it.[3] Paul just finished saying that he did not lose heart even though the outer man was wasting away. Here he developed some further reasons why he didn't lose heart in the face of physical deterioration.

These reasons illustrate Paul's motivations for service. And they remain valid motivations for us today. These reasons include the assurance of a new body, the motivation of a new goal, the reality of judgment, the power of Christ's love, and the significance of Christ's sacrifice.

The Assurance of a New Body (1-6)

Paul did not lose heart in the face of the situations that he outlined in 2 Corinthians 4:8-10 because he knew the temporary nature of the physical body that was being hard pressed, perplexed, persecuted, struck down, and was deteriorating. Even if the body had been destroyed, so what? Life would not have ended! In fact, the destruction of the physical body is merely the doorway to something better—to the post-resurrection body.

Paul mentioned several contrasts between the "now" body and the "not yet" body.

---

[3]*Gar* is the same word used to introduce the discussion in 2 Corinthians 1:12. See the discussion on that verse, page 34.

The Now Body	The Not Yet Body
Tent	Building
Earthly	In Heaven
Is Destroyed	Eternal
Built by Human Hands	From God

When Paul described our present body as an "earthly tent," he was stressing the temporary nature of our body. Not only is it temporary, but it is not as stable as a building. A tent can be blown away. A tent is quite movable. A tent has no foundation to it, but a building is solid, more stable, founded, and lasting.

The environment of our present body is an "earthly" environment; so it is susceptible to any problem that this earth can bring to it. It is a temporary body presently going through destruction. As a matter of fact, our physical body begins a process of dying as soon as it begins the process of living. Every person who has lived very long understands this. We spend a lot of energy and money keeping the body pumped up.

When Paul talked about our present body's being built by human hands, he did not mean that God is not a part of this world. He was referring to the fact that no one is born into this world without human initiation. One's present body is a combination of the genes and chromosomes that come from both the mother and the father. The resurrected body does not come from humanness. Rather, it comes totally from God's design. Because God is eternal, the new body has nothing temporary about it.

Notice that the new body has a new permanence (building), a new environment (in Heaven), a new source (from God). No wonder Paul intensely desired a new body, "Meanwhile we groan, longing to be clothed with our heavenly dwelling" (2 Corinthians 5:2).

But just what was Paul getting at when he talked about being "clothed" and not being "found naked"? What did he mean when he said, "We do not wish to be unclothed but to be clothed"?

Paul was correcting some philosophical Greek thought of the first century. The Greeks taught that the body was evil, and man's chief aim was to be without a body. They taught that the spirit had to be set free from the body because the body was imprisoning and limiting the spirit.

For the Jews and for the Christians, that is a horrible picture. We rightly understand that the body of man and the man himself cannot be separated, for to deprive a person from his body is to deprive a person from his personality. Without a body, we would just be a shadow existing. After all, it is through the body that human relationships are made and maintained. No one can relate well to a disembodied spirit just floating around in loneliness and isolation. Relationships cannot be formed without a body. Man's spirit needs a body and man's body needs a spirit. Christians do not look for the time when they will have *no* body, but rather for a time when they will have a *new* body. To be free from the body is to be "unclothed." It would be for the spirit to be "naked." But instead of that, we are going to be further clothed, because the mortal will put on immortality. While the Greeks looked to be unclothed from the body—that is, to have no body—the Christians refused that kind of thinking. So the word *clothed* refers to putting on a new body. The word *naked* refers to being without a body. It is true that many of the problems that we have are connected with our temporary physical bodies. We experience pain because our bodies get hurt. We experience fatigue because our bodies get tired. We can experience emotional changes when certain chemicals in our bodies get out of balance. We experience discomfort when our bodies get too hot or too cold. Consequently, many people in the first century thought the way to solve all those problems was to have no body at all. Let the spirit become "naked," for the only function of the body was to put some kind of skin clothing around the spirit. So the desire was to escape from the body and thus from life's disappointments.

For the Christian, the issue is not escape, but transformation. Instead of trying to have no body, Paul made it clear that we are created to have an eternal body—"Now it is God who has made us for this very purpose" (2 Corinthians 5:5). That is, He has made us for the purpose of having a body that will never cease to exist and will never be threatened or have problems because of its environment. Our new body is made for Heaven, and Heaven is being prepared to receive our new bodies. God has given us a guarantee that we are made for this purpose. That guarantee is the Holy Spirit. That is God's first down payment of everything He will give us in Heaven.

The Holy Spirit in us begins the transformation process (2 Corinthians 3:18). We are now in the process of being transformed on the inside. That's what Paul meant when he said that "inwardly we are being renewed day by day" (2 Corinthians 4:16).

The Holy Spirit equips us with the kind of characteristics and conduct that will dominate our Heavenly existence. At a later time, we will receive a body that corresponds to that Spirit. But with the coming of the Holy Spirit, already a taste of God's future has invaded our present existence. With the coming of the Holy Spirit, we have already tasted something of the life that is to come (Hebrews 6:5).

Life in This Body (6-10)

Instead of trying to escape from this body, the assurance that the Christian is made to live eternally and will receive a new body causes him to take on new perspectives for living in this body. In this paragraph, several of those perspectives are mentioned:

1. Courage: "We are always confident."
2. Faith: "We live by faith."
3. Purpose: "We make it our goal to please him."
4. Future judgment: "For we must all appear before the judgment seat of Christ."

Paul had confidence, because he not only saw the present time, but also the future. People were created to be future-oriented, and what we anticipate in the future determines how we live our lives in the present. That's why Jesus had confidence even though He was being misunderstood, ridiculed, rejected, betrayed, tried, and taken to the cross. During His lifetime, He spoke about the future. He not only talked about the fact that He was going to be crucified, but also the fact that He was going to be raised from the dead. He had the "big picture." And with the big picture in His mind, the little details, as uncomfortable and as undesirable and as painful as they were, did not discourage Him. He was able to see through the little pieces to the big picture. And the big picture was characterized by victory, eternal life, and reunion with the Father.

That was what Paul was getting at when he said that "we live by faith, not by sight" (2 Corinthians 5:7). It is true that there is some distraction while living in this present body, but the distraction is far overweighed by the attraction of being totally with the Lord in the future. Paul was getting at that when he wrote elsewhere that, "I consider that our present sufferings are not worth comparing with the glory that will be revealed in us" (Romans 8:18).

When Paul mentioned that we are "away from the Lord" when we are "at home in the body," he did not mean a total distancing from the Lord while we are living in this physical body on planet earth. For elsewhere he affirmed the Lord's presence. In fact, he just finished saying that the Lord has given us His Spirit as a deposit. He mentioned in 1 Corinthians 6:19 that the body is the temple of the Holy Spirit "who is in you." When the Spirit is in us, then the Lord is in us for "the Lord is the Spirit" (2 Corinthians 3:17).

Paul never sensed that a Christian is totally "away from the Lord." In fact, Jesus himself promised, "I am with you always" (Matthew 28:20). So what was Paul getting at when he said that when we are at home in the body (meaning in this world with our physical bodies), we are "away from the Lord"? He was talking about being away from the *Heavenly presence* of the Lord. It is clear that one day we shall be *totally* in the presence of the Lord, "for we shall see him as he is" (1 John 3:2). It is clear that Paul was talking about that "sight" presence of the Lord because he immediately picked that up in the next verse: "We live by faith, not by sight." At one time, the apostles were in the presence of Jesus' resurrected body, and Jesus said to them, "Because you have seen me, you have believed; blessed are those who have not seen and yet have believed" (John 20:29).

While we are in this body, we are away from seeing the Lord; so we live by faith. Of course, we are all looking forward to the time when we will be able to see Him. And we prefer that (2 Corinthians 5:8). Although we prefer it, we do not make that such a priority that we cop out on living here on earth in this body for our Lord. It was not Paul's environment, whether in this body or in the eternal body, that determined his life. Rather it was Paul's goal. And Paul's goal was to please the Lord in whatever environment he found himself (2 Corinthians 5:9). That goal was Paul's motivation for service.

A part of that goal was the realization that every person will appear before the judgment seat of Christ (2 Corinthians 5:10). Christians will not be judged for their sins, but rather for their services in their human bodies. We will be judged by whether or not we have really been people helpers. Have we stopped to help

81

people in need as the Samaritan, or have we walked by to the other side?

Our sensitivity to the needs of people, our services in light of those needs, and the use of our various abilities for the benefit of others will determine whether we have done "good or bad" in this body. That will determine whether or not we have been pleasing to Him. This concept of doing "good or bad" in our physical bodies really contradicted Greek thought, for the Greeks believed that nothing good could be done through an "evil" body. But Paul made it clear that God will judge what is done *in* the body. Of course the first criterion for judgment will be in our relationship with Christ—our rootage. But we will also be judged by our fruit-age. (See Matthew 25:31 and following.) The judgment will be more of an announcing for the Christian than a "judging." The judging is *now* taking place.

There are several activities in which we should be involved in the face of the coming judgment. Paul mentioned some of those in this chapter, including fearing God (2 Corinthians 5:11a), persuading men (2 Corinthians 5:11b), and unselfish activity (2 Corinthians 5:12, 13).

The judgment will be fair but tough. There are several aspects of the judgment. Here are some of them:

1. We will be judged with the same judgment that we have given out on earth (Matthew 7:1). If we have not forgiven others, we will not be forgiven (Matthew 6:14).

2. We will be judged by our involvement in meeting the needs of humanity (Matthew 25:31-46).

3. We will be judged by our words (Matthew 12:36).

4. We will be judged by our deeds (2 Corinthians 5:10).

5. We will be judged by our obedience of God's will for our lives (Matthew 7:21).

6. We will be judged by the Word (John 12:48).

7. We will be judged without mercy if we have shown no mercy (James 2:13).

8. We will be judged by our position in Christ (John 3:16-18; 1 John 5:12, 13).

9. The judgment will be true and pure. It will be accurate and without partiality. There will be no mixed motives with God (Revelation 19:2).

10. We will be judged in accordance with the *charisma* God has given us to use. We must not evaluate ourselves by others.

Whatever we have—our capabilities and potential are God-given. He has put us in this body (the church), and He lives in our bodies (our temporary earthly tents) in accordance with His wisdom so that He can have the use of our bodies for serving mankind. He expects us to be involved for His name's sake.

There are several insights about the judgment from 2 Corinthians 5:10. Here they are:

1. It is a must: "For we *must* all appear. . . ."

2. It is universal: "We must *all* appear. . . ." No one will be able to miss the judgment.

3. It is personal: ". . . that *each one* may receive what is due." There will be no mass reward or mass punishment. God will deal with us as individuals.

4. It will be fair: "before the judgment seat of Christ."

5. It will be a judgment of our practices, not just of our position: "for the things done while in the body."

6. It will not be prejudiced: "whether good or bad."

7. There will be a payback: "that each one may receive what is due him."

The Christian should not fear this judgment, but rather welcome it. Remember that the Holy Spirit has been given to us as a guarantee of what is to come—and God does not give us the Spirit as a guarantee that we are going to be singed. The Spirit is given to us as God's presence on earth as a guarantee that we will be in His presence in Heaven forever. That is why the Christian "may be confident and unashamed before him at his coming" (1 John 2:28; cf. 4:17).

We will have confidence on the day of judgment. Judging for the Christian will not be to determine whether or not we are in the family of God. We are *in* the family of God because we are *in* Christ. The judging for the Christian will be an evaluation of how well we have lived out our responsibility in the family. It will be a determinate for our rewards. No parents evaluate their children to determine whether or not they are in the family. Those children are in the family by birth. We evaluate their maturity, their usefulness, their responsibility, and their cooperation.

Paul did not want us just to sit around in our physical bodies waiting for the big escape. He wanted us to be responsible and to serve mankind in our physical bodies even as Jesus did in His physical body. Jesus knew that His body was temporary. He knew He would die an early death, but that did not keep Him from reaching out to touch people with the love of God. God expects us to invest our lives into the lives of others. Parents do that, knowing full well that the children will be out of the home in a few years. And we must do that with other people, knowing full well that we will be out of our "house" (our body) in a few years.

The Motivation of Fearing the Lord (11-13)

Fearing God does not mean having a terror of God, but rather a respect for God. It means having an awe of God. Out of knowing God, respecting God, and exalting God with an unquenchable awe, the Christian persuades others. What is it that Christians should persuade other people about? They should persuade others about the nature of God, the potential reconciliation of man to God, the usefulness of man in Christ, and the destiny of history—toward the judgment seat of Christ.

We Christians are not to persuade non-Christians about the value of ourselves, but rather about the value of the Lord. Too many times, a congregation spends most of its energy trying to convince people of the value of that particular church when what we need to do is to turn the eyes of people toward the Lord.

The false teachers were interested in their own achievements. They spotlighted their own achievements so that people would follow them because of their appearances. Paul did not show off in front of the people. He gave them some valid reasons for having confidence in him, but those reasons dealt with spirituality, not superficial status.

Many people do not understand that kind of humble life-style. They think that is the life-style of someone who is out of his right mind, for we live in a world where people exist to pull their own strings, to get ahead of others, to elevate self, to purposely position self to receive approvals. If a person refuses to do this, he is believed to be rather crazy.

People thought Jesus was off His rocker because He would not take advantage of His power to benefit himself. Jesus refused to do that when the devil tempted Him in the wilderness for forty days, and He expects us to refuse to do that, also.

The Motivation of Christ's Love (14, 15)

The word *compels* is from a Greek word that literally means "holds together." It is Christ's love that keeps the Christian from falling apart in the midst of a world that does not understand him.

It is Christ's love that keeps the Christian from quitting when he is not appreciated. It is Christ's love that keeps the Christian committed to being involved in a ministry for the benefit of others. It is clear in this text that Paul was not motivated out of a fear of the judgment, but rather out of a respect for Christ's love. While Paul had a desire to leave planet earth and be in the total presence of Jesus, it was Christ's love that kept him committed to live out his life on earth for the benefit of others.

Christ's love is comprehensive. It refers to the love Christ had for Paul. It also refers to the love Paul had for Christ, and it also refers to the love that Christ puts inside the hearts of all Christians. For God's love has been poured into our hearts through the Holy Spirit (Romans 5:5). But primarily, *Christ's love* here refers to the love Christ has for all mankind, as seen in His sacrifice, for He died for all.

This is a pivotal truth for Paul. Prior to being convinced that Christ had died for *all,* Paul hated Christ and sought to oppose everything He stood for. When Paul encountered the risen Christ on the road to Damascus, he rightly knew that He had died for Paul as well as for other people. Christ's death was a substitutionary death. He died for all, because all had died in sin, and Christ took our sin inside of His body. He took our sentence for us. He took our separation from the Father for us.

The obedience of Christ on the cross has its counterpart in the obligation of man on earth. As Christ died for man, man must live for Christ. We are no longer to live for ourselves, but for Him. And what does it mean to live for Him? It means that we enter into a ministry of reconciliation.

God has called us to privilege and purpose. Privilege is what He does for us; Christ died for us. But purpose is what He expects from us; He expects for us to be His servants—to be people helpers. And by being people helpers, we can be God's ambassadors, bringing people to God through Jesus Christ.

And that is what Paul immediately turned his attention to in the following verses.

Practices of Service (5:16-21)

Our practice of service involves several aspects, including a proper perspective, a proper position, a proper responsibility, a proper representation, and a proper righteousness.

A New Perspective (16)

The first way a Christian lives for Christ is by viewing people differently. We are no longer to view people from just outward appearance. We are no longer to view people from the standpoint of their status. We are no longer to view people in the way the world views people. We need to view people with value. We need to view people with potential. We need to view people with possibility. We need to view people as those for whom Christ died because Jesus still loves them. When Christ died for all, He put a high premium on every person. That estimate of people from Jesus put an end to Paul's seeing man from a human standpoint only, and it should also put an end to our superficial evaluations.

We have a tendency to evaluate man from external distinctions only—like race, class, wealth, sex, occupation, health. Now those meant nothing to Paul, and they are to mean nothing to us. If everyone was in Christ's purpose on the cross, then everyone is worthy to be loved, saved, and served. Paul was big enough to look beyond the people's situations to see the potential of people in Christ, and so must we!

Too many churches have sections of town where they will not minister nor seek to evangelize. It is time that we call a moratorium on that practice and see people from Heaven's viewpoint. At one time, Paul had viewed Christ from just a human perspective. He had seen Christ as a human blasphemer, an enemy of God, a heretical teacher, a political messiah, a cursed man. And there are people today who view Christ from just a human perspective. They see Him as a mere prophet, a mere teacher, a good moral man, or a political superstar, but not the divine Son of God who was indeed God in flesh. No Christian can seek to serve the Lord well unless he changes the way he looks at people.

A New Position (17)

A Christian must not only view others differently, but he must also view himself differently if he is going to be God's servant. Christians are in a new position. Christians are "in Christ." In Christ, a Christian is a new creation; so a Christian must view himself with better esteem than many Christians have. A Christian must view his past differently. A Christian can no longer hang on to the past. Whether that past has been bad or good, the Christian must let go of it so that the Spirit of Christ can fill him to usefulness now and in the future.

Too many Christians have concreted themselves to their sinful past. They will not move out to serve because they are too filled with guilt. On the cross, Jesus forgave us. That guilt is taken away. Christians are no longer guilty in Christ.

Some Christians continue to look back to the past of their good experiences. It seems they are always wanting to go back to something former that was better. The Israelites thought like that. After God brought them out of Egypt, many times they complained and wanted to get back to the "good ole days." Many Christians who move from one location to another never really get involved in their new location because they are always thinking about how great it was where they previously lived. They dream about how great the church was, how great the people were, and how great the opportunities were. We must not ponder the things of the past in order to keep our minds, our commitment, our emotions, and our service back there. We must be free from the past in order to be used in the present and in order to face our lives towards future service for God.

What is some of the old that has passed away? Paul mentioned several things, including the old motives (2 Corinthians 5:14), a life lived for self (2 Corinthians 5:15), the old way of looking at people (2 Corinthians 5:16), the old way of looking at Christ (2 Corinthians 5:16), a life of isolation and alienation (2 Corinthians 5:18), and a life of meaninglessness (2 Corinthians 5:19).

A New Responsibility (18, 19)

Again we see that God has called us to both privilege and purpose. The privilege is what He has done for us. He has reconciled us to himself through Jesus Christ, for Christ died for our sins. How did that happen? God poured our sins into Christ on the cross. So Christ took our wrap. He became guilty for us. He took the responsibility for our sins. And in Christ, God forgives us. But with that privilege comes purpose! God gives to us "the ministry of reconciliation." Every Christian is to be involved in a ministry of reconciliation by the abilities that God has given to him. We are to be living vessels pointing people to God. In Christ, God made it clear that He does not keep score on man's sins. In Christ, God forgives man. He does not hold sin against us. But He does hold something up to us. He holds up to us the message of reconciliation, which He expects to come out of us to others.

He expects the Christian who has been saved to be interested in saving others. He expects the beggar who has found bread to be interested in telling other beggars where that bread can be located. If one does not accept that ministry, then that one has rejected God's New Covenant.

A New Representative (20)

God has called us to be His stand-in representatives for the rest of mankind who are alive during our lifetimes. The word *ambassador* is a word that refers to an emperor's messenger. He acted in the place of the emperor. He was the emperor's stand-in. An ambassador could not be independent. He could not speak in his own name, act in his own way, or communicate his own ideas. In a sense, he brought the presence of the emperor to the people by sharing the emperor's message.

And that's what God expects every Christian to do. This is not just the task of the ordained. It is the task of the baptized, for God is "making his appeal through us" (2 Corinthians 5:20). And if we are not open for another with God's reconciling love, then God's appeal is not made. This appeal is part of God's way of saving men, and men are not saved without it.

For faith comes from hearing and hearing by the Word of God (Romans 10:17). Some people believe that people are automatically saved because Christ died on the cross, but that is not the teaching of the Bible. If all people are automatically saved because of Christ's act, then there would be no need for the next verses. There would be no need for the New Testament. There would have been no need for Paul to have ministered in Corinth. Men are not saved just because Christ died any more than people in another country who have never heard of aspirin can lower their fevers just because we have aspirin that is spoiling on the shelves in this country. There must be a connection.

Our ministry of reconciliation is not limited to reconciling the lost to God. It also includes reconciling people to one another. A "ministry of reconciliation" presupposes that there has been some kind of separation, alienation, or rift of friendship.

This world is filled with people who need reconciliation with other people. Walk into a kitchen and listen to parents scream at their teenagers and teenagers scream at their parents. They need a ministry of reconciliation. Walk into a living room and observe a husband and wife who do not speak to one another for three or four hours. They need a word of reconciliation. Walk into a church board meeting and hear the secret thoughts of elders or deacons who are thinking, "If we just had another preacher, we would go somewhere." And then listen to the secret thoughts of the preacher who may be thinking, "If we just had new elders or deacons, we might go somewhere." Those leaders need a ministry of reconciliation.

Observe the unmarried teenager in a Christian home who discovers she is pregnant. She needs a word of reconciliation.

Christians are to be God's first-class mail by sharing with both the non-Christian and the Christian a ministry of reconciliation.

Jesus majored in that kind of ministry. He reached out to people who were angry, greedy, lonely, afraid, and stigmatized. He spoke in a way that touched their hearts and ministered to their feelings. He brought a word of reconciliation and lived out services of reconciliation. And He says to His followers, "Follow Me."

God expects us to be His representatives, and He deserves it! Isn't He a good enough God for us to represent? Of course, He is. But some may say, "But I am not good enough to represent God." Paul dealt with that in the next verse.

A New Righteousness (21)

Paul would not allow anyone to think that he was not good enough to represent God. Every Christian is, because God has given every Christian a new righteousness. That has come because our sins are forgiven and forgotten. And God puts within us the Holy Spirit. We are not perfect, but we are forgiven! We are acquitted! We are clean!

The word *righteousness* involves both an acquittal, which is God's forgiveness, and an equipment, which is God's provision for us to live out a life for Him. God gives us the Holy Spirit as equipment. God gives us the church as equipment. God gives us His Word as equipment.

Summary

What have we learned from this chapter?

1. The Christian should not try to escape from a body.

2. Our temporary bodies will be replaced by eternal ones.

3. God has made us to be eternal people and He has given us the Holy Spirit as the first taste of our eternal life.

4. We live by faith.

5. Our goal is to please God whether we are here on earth or in Heaven.

6. We will appear before the judgment seat of Christ.

7. It is out of deep respect for the Lord that we persuade men to be reconciled to God.

8. We do not preach ourselves, but Christ.

9. It is Christ's love that keeps us committed to being His servants.

10. Christ died for all because all had died.

11. Christ died for us so that we could live for Him.

12. We are to see people from a different perspective.

13. We are to see ourselves from a different perspective—a new creation.

14. We are to let go of the past so we can fill the present with God's purpose.

15. God has given us both privilege—what He has done for us—and purpose—what He expects from us. (See below.)

16. Christians are God's ambassadors—God's stand-ins.

17. God makes His appeal through us to other people, or that appeal is not made at all.

18. God has made us righteous for the task by forgiving us our sins and giving us the Holy Spirit.

To receive God's New Covenant is to receive both His privilege and His purpose. That means we are to be involved in a ministry of reconciliation. If we are not involved in a ministry of reconciliation with the gifts that God has given to us, then we have received God's grace in vain.

Paul turned to that subject in the next chapter.

CHAPTER SIX

Practices of People Helpers

2 Corinthians 6:1—7:1

From Paul's perspective, there was no break between the end of 2 Corinthians 5 and the beginning of chapter 6. In chapter 5, he developed the fact that God has called us to both a position—new creatures in Christ—and also to a practice—being ambassadors of God. God calls people to be His ambassadors so that He can make His appeal through us. He has called us to be His "fellow workers." So Paul began chapter 6 affirming that this was precisely what he was doing. He was "God's fellow worker." But Paul immediately moved to what he wanted the Corinthians to do. He wanted the Corinthians also to be God's fellow workers.

Priorities of People Helpers (6:1-3)

As God has helped us in Christ, He expects us to help others. We are to be people helpers. That is why Paul urged the Corinthians "not to receive God's grace in vain" (2 Corinthians 6:1). God's grace involves responsibility on the part of those who receive it. In the context of 2 Corinthians 5, out of which this immediately flows, the *grace* refers to what God has done for the Corinthians, both in putting them in a new position and in giving them a practice of responsibility. This *grace* refers to the following:
1. Jesus' sacrifice for us and its purpose (2 Corinthians 5:15),
2. becoming a new creation (2 Corinthians 5:17),
3. the passing of the old and the coming of the new (2 Corinthians 5:17),
4. reconciliation to God (2 Corinthians 5:18),
5. receiving the ministry of reconciliation (2 Corinthians 5:18),
6. receiving the message of reconciliation (2 Corinthians 5:19),
7. being an ambassador of God (2 Corinthians 5:20), and
8. becoming the righteousness of God (2 Corinthians 5:21).

So God's grace does not refer just to what God has done for us, but also to the ministry that God has given to us. It is grace on God's part to share with us His activities and ministry for others. Anytime anyone of more status asks us to become a partner with him—to do with him what he wants to do—that is grace.

The apostle Paul, in other places, referred to grace as being the responsibility that God had given to him. "Surely you have heard about the administration of God's grace that was given to me for you" (Ephesians 3:2). "I became a servant of this gospel by the gift of God's grace given me through the working of his power" (Ephesians 3:7). "By the grace God has given me, I laid a foundation as an expert builder . . ." (1 Corinthians 3:10).

How, then, could the Corinthians receive God's grace in vain? First, they could receive the benefits of Christ's sacrifice but continue to live for themselves. Or, while they were actually a new creation, they could continue to live selfishly as the old creation did. Third, although "the new has come" (2 Corinthians 5:17), they could fail to live out that newness as people helpers. Fourth, since they had received the "ministry of reconciliation" (2 Corinthians 5:18) by God's grace, to fail to reach out in such a ministry would have been to receive that grace in vain. The same is true for the "message of reconciliation" (2 Corinthians 5:19). Not to share that message with others would mean they had received that grace in vain. By God's grace, they were "Christ's ambassadors" (2 Corinthians 5:20), but not to allow God to make His appeal through them would have been, once again, receiving God's grace in vain. Finally, they would have received God's grace in vain if, since they had received the "righteousness of God" through Christ (2 Corinthians 5:21), they were not expressing that righteousness in proper relationships with others. In other words, to "receive God's grace in vain" is to receive Christ's death, but not appropriate His life as people helpers.

Since God had done His part to bring people to himself, He then expected the Corinthians to do their part and use what He had given to them in a right way. That way was being a people helper. But the Corinthians had not been doing a good job at that. Instead of being in a ministry of reconciliation, they were spreading a ministry of revenge as they were caught up in competition with one another and complaints against one another. Instead of living for others, they lived for themselves. The old things had not passed away from the way they were treating each other. They were evaluating people from externals. They were even beginning to evaluate Christ from a human point of view (1 Corinthians 15). With God's grace always comes *charisma,* but *charisma* is always given for the purpose of making the recipient a people helper.

To receive God's grace in vain is to receive God's gifts but to waste those gifts. That's what Paul was getting at in 1 Corinthians 3:12-15. He was restating his case here. To receive God's grace in vain is to do "bad" with those gifts (2 Corinthians 5:10). To do bad with those gifts is to do nothing that would bring other people closer to the Lord and to each other.

The opposite of receiving God's grace in vain is receiving God's grace with fruitfulness. In 2 Corinthians 6:2, Paul gave a reason for wanting the Corinthians to accept God's responsibility with fruitfulness. He quoted from Isaiah 49:8, "In the time of my favor I heard you, and in the day of salvation I helped you." Then Paul said, "Now is the time of God's favor, now is the day of salvation." The quotation from Isaiah is from one of the "suffering servant" passages in Isaiah. Those suffering servant passages deal with the fact that God has called someone to be His people helper. The context in Isaiah deals with Israel's responsibility to serve in a ministry of reconciliation; but Israel did not do it; so Jesus would come to do it. Now that Jesus has come, God called a new Israel to continue being involved in a ministry of reconciliation.

When people accept God's call to salvation, they also accept God's call to service. The two go together. Paul quoted from the same chapter in Isaiah (verse 6) in Acts 13:47: "I have made you a light for the Gentiles, that you may bring salvation to the ends of the earth." There it was Jews who should have turned to the Gentiles, but they did not, so Paul reminded them of their irresponsibility, contrasting it with God's responsibility.

Regardless of our situation in life, we are to be people helpers for God, and God will help us in it. To say that "now is the time of God's favor, now is the day of salvation," is not saying that now is the day to receive salvation by sanctification, but rather to express it by service. Paul was writing to those who had already received salvation by sanctification. What they needed to do was express it. That's what he had been getting at ever since 2 Corinthians 5:11. It is when we express it that others can receive the benefits of God's salvation. Therefore, *now* is the time to express it.

Paul was calling the Corinthians to take on the priority of being people helpers. He himself had taken that responsibility seriously by not putting a stumbling block in anyone's path so that his ministry would not be discredited (2 Corinthians 6:3). Paul did not want to get in the way of other people progressing in their walk with the Lord. How would other people stumble over Paul's particular ministry? Three possibilities seem apparent from the way Paul developed the rest of this chapter:

1. People might stumble if they observed Paul's responding with a negative reaction in difficult situations (2 Corinthians 6:4-10).

2. They might stumble if Paul displayed a hostile relationship to fellow Christians (2 Corinthians 6:11-13).

3. They might stumble if Paul caved in to the life-style of non-Christians with whom he associated (2 Corinthians 6:14—7:1).

Being involved in a ministry of reconciliation is to become vulnerable, for no one can be in a ministry of reconciliation without having relationships with people. People will observe us. What they observe can either help them as a stepping stone toward a closer walk with the Lord or be a stumbling block that puts a wall between them and the Lord. Each of us needs to seek to be stepping stones in our reactions in difficult situations, our relationships with other Christians, and our practices when associating with non-Christians.

Pressures of People Helpers (6:4-10)

Being a people helper is not a life of ease. A people helper does not buy a rocker-recliner and then rock himself into serenity for the rest of his life. Difficult times will come, but God's people helpers must commit themselves in those difficult times to being people helpers. Paul's umbrella words that showed how he handled those difficult times are "in great endurance" (2 Corinthians 6:4). The word *endurance* comes from a Greek word that literally means to "remain under." The idea is to remain under a difficult situation rather than to run from it. Paul then described several different kinds of situations under which he had remained.

Paul first gave a general description of those difficult situations with the words, "troubles, hardships and distresses." The word for *troubles* is the Greek word θλίψις (*thlipsis*), discussed above. It stresses severe pressure. The pressure could be physical, mental, social, spiritual, or all of these combined. The word *hardships* deals with necessities in life—primarily financial difficulties. Paul knew how to live "in want" (Philippians 4:12). To mention this situation violates the idea that God will provide all kinds of financial rewards if we just get on the bandwagon and serve Him better. God did not promise that to Jesus. Jesus did not have a place to lay His head. Jesus lived in material poverty, although all of His necessities were taken care of. The word *distresses* literally means "no room to turn around." It describes a situation that is frustrating and can lead to depression. It might well describe a person in a room where all four walls are closing in on him while at the same time the ceiling and the floor are moving toward each other. There does not seem to be any way out.

These three words stress the vulnerability of a people helper. Being a people helper can replace ease with pressure, surplus with economical needs (because it may cost money out of our own pocket to help people), and freedom with no place to turn around. Haven't you noticed that when people need your help, they are very demanding and often leave you no room to do anything else with your life except to reach out and help them? They can eat up all your time, your priorities, your money, your freedom, and your energy. That's what it means to be in a situation where there is not much room to turn around.

One problem within the church is that some of us try to figure out the conclusion before we get involved in helping people. We try to avoid those situations that are really going to be demanding on us. It is easy to spend energy living for ourselves, keeping the church building open and attending the meetings. But it is not so easy to reach out to meet the needs of others. The beauty of Jesus is that He headed straight into those kinds of situations because people were there who needed help. He turned His face to the cross, knowing that the cross would hurt. He refused to live His life trying to protect and keep it.

Next Paul moved to some specific troubles that he had experienced even as Jesus had. Those specific troubles may be grouped under two categories: (a) troubles that come from others—beatings, imprisonments, and riots—and (b) troubles that one gives to himself—hard work, sleepless nights, and hunger.

The beatings describe every kind of beating—beatings with both rods and whips. Paul was beaten so severely early in his ministry that he wrote about the fact that he bore on his body the marks of Jesus. At least five times he received thirty-nine lashes from the Jews (2 Corinthians 11:24). Paul's body must have been covered with scars. He was not a pretty sight to behold.

Paul was an ex-convict, for he had spent time in prison. Not only did he spend one time in prison, but he was a repeater. In fact, he said that he had been in prison "more frequently" than others (2 Corinthians 11:23). Paul also was the object of several riots.

We look at a person today who may be so rejected by society that he literally has rocks thrown at him, is hit over the head, has his car beat on, and is often put in jail because where that person is, riots are all around him. When we see such a person, it is easy to think that he is not as mature as he ought to be. Many people thought that about Martin Luther King, Jr., as he was involved in a significant ministry. But let us be careful, for that describes the life of the apostle Paul. Paul suggested that this could happen to anyone who is really involved in being a people helper. Ambassadors for God are not appreciated by the ambassadors of the devil, and the ambassadors of the devil have a lot of partners to oppose God's people.

There were several difficult times that Paul inflicted upon himself. These are "hard work, sleepless nights and hunger." The word for *hard work* is from a Greek word that literally means a "severe cutting fatigue." Is it possible that too many of us are lazy and will not expend energy if we are really going to get worn out doing the work of the Lord? Paul's cutting fatigue involved both his work as an evangelist and as a wage-earner, for many times he worked as a tentmaker while also being a people helper. The church can never grow if members will not accept fatiguing work. We spend more time watching television commercials than being involved as people helpers. Being a real people helper can cause us to lose sleep in more ways than one. It may cause us to go to bed late and get up early because we are helping people. It can also cause us to toss and turn with insomnia because we have someone's problems on our minds. It can also cause us to lose sleep because we are praying for situations and people in those situations. We will lose sleep for partying; how about losing sleep for praying? Being a people helper can also bring hunger to God's ambassador, and that can happen in various ways also. The hunger can result from a voluntary fasting because we are so involved in God's work that we literally forget to eat. It can also result through a planned prolonged fasting for the purpose of praying and meditating. Being a real people helper in the name of God can also cause us to go hungry because we spend the money we have for food to help someone else in need and thus have no money left over. It can also cause us to go hungry because we may lose our job since we refuse to cave in to the expectations of a pagan employer who wants us to be dishonest. Does God's work ever cut into our eating?

How can anyone endure that kind of life-style? The answer to that lies in an inner disposition (2 Corinthians 6:6, 7). Right after Paul talked about the outer distress, he followed that up with a discussion of the inner disposition necessary to live through the outer distress.

The circumstances that are a discomfort are accompanied by characteristics that are divine. Paul mentions several of those characteristics here:

1. Purity. Purity does not refer to being sinless. Rather it describes one who is cleansed and is sincere about his life after that cleaning. He continues to keep his life morally clean. He does not want to be a dirty lamp for God's light. He does not want to be a dirty container for God's treasure.

2. Understanding. An understanding person can live through difficulties because he knows what—or Who—"stands under" those difficulties. God stands under those difficulties. And God will hold him up during those difficult times.

3. Patience. The Greek word for *patience* here refers to putting up with difficult people. This kind of person can receive irritation from other people without getting angry or taking revenge. Such an attitude leads to the next characteristic.

4. Kindness. Love is kind, not blind. Love sees the difficulties in other people, but is tall enough to look over those difficulties and see that those people are people of worth. So the people helper reaches out to those whom God loves because they are worthy of being helped in the name of God. A person who is kind does to others what he would want them to do for him, regardless of whether or not they would ever do it for him. The person who is kind knows what it means to overcome evil with good.

5. The Holy Spirit. The Holy Spirit is the source of the power of the inner disposition necessary to live in an alien world. The godly disposition comes from the divine source—the Holy Spirit—not from a human source. The fruit of the Spirit (Galatians 5:22, 23) feeds the inner disposition with the soul food it needs to live through all that is involved in being a people helper.

6. *Sincere love.* The word *sincere* refers to genuine love. Sincere love is not a "phony baloney" kind of love. It does not discriminate or seek a return for its own benefit. Sincere love seeks the success of the other person. A sincere love loves a person who is not a brother as a brother. Sincere love loves a person who is not a friend as a friend. Sincere love does not love preaching without loving people. Sincere love is not counterfeit. It expresses itself in truth.

7. *Truthful speech.* Truth and love are close together. In fact, we are to speak God's truth in love (Ephesians 4:15). Truthful speech is vital for, and a part of, significant fellowship. One description of Christian fellowship is Christ in people benefiting people in Christ. Thus, the use of truthful speech will never be used to mean that we say anything that can hurt someone else just because it is the truth. We need to be stewards of our words. Our words need to build people up, not tear them down. Our words need to be filled with grace that can minister to a person in that person's need. Sticks and stones can break my bones, but words can kill the spirit and the soul!

8. *The power of God.* No person can live the kind of disposition that Paul outlined without the inner presence of God himself empowering that person. It is the power of God that overcomes evil.

In a sense, every one of the above character dispositions is the power of God. Purity is the power of God. The Holy Spirit, sincere love, and truthful speech are the power of God. All of those are the power of God because all of those come from God. The opposite of every one of those are ways in which man tries to live through situations in his own power. That's the difference between the impotence of man and the power of God.

9. *Weapons of righteousness.* Man is not to live through the circumstances of life with the same kinds of warfare attitudes and activities that the pagan have and express. Instead, we are to live through difficult situations with God's equipment. In the sixth chapter of Ephesians, Paul listed the weapons that the Christian is to use during this cosmic warfare. In fact, Paul connected those weapons with the fact that he was "an ambassador" (Ephesians 6:20). Consequently, the weapons Paul outlined in Ephesians 6 are the specifics of the weapons he mentions here; they are the weapons for God's ambassador.

When Paul mentioned "in the right hand and in the left," he meant he was not vacillating. It didn't make any difference which direction he turned, he was going to use the same weapons. Today, the words *right* and *left* refer to liberalism and conservativism. Some people like to vacillate between the two and display a different character when relating to those on his right from what he displays when he relates to those on his left. But the Christian character is not for compromise.

The right hand and left hand were significant in another way, also. The two were used in battle in specific ways. A person carried his sword in the right hand, and for the Christian the sword of the Spirit is the Word of God. A person held his shield in his left hand, and for the Christian, our shield is faith. So the Christian combines trust in God with the Word of God for living through the difficult situations in life. He answers difficult situations with the Word of God, but he cannot answer that if he does not know the Word of God. And we cannot know the Word of God if we continue to spend more time in front of the television than we spend in the Word.

The Christian also lives through the difficult times through trust in God, who is more powerful than any of the "giants" that the world can send to us. Without the Word and without trust, the Christian has little staying power in the midst of difficult times that will come as he is helping people.

After Paul discussed difficult times in both general and specific terms, he then moved to talk about difficult times that come through being misrepresented. Paul summed up the range of negative attitudes that people had toward him (2 Corinthians 6:8-10). Fewer people have been more misunderstood than Jesus and Paul. But any time a person in the name of Christ reaches out to help another, he is open to being misunderstood. Paul was misunderstood by those people who judged superficially. Christians must be willing to minister without calculating or manipulating the kind of response they are going to receive. Paul summed up the kind of response he had with the words *glory* and *dishonor.* Christians will always get mixed reviews; the responses to their message will be different in different situations. But the message must remain the same, in spite of the response.

Paul listed several responses (2 Corinthians 6:8-10) that serve as encouragement to us:

"Good report"—some people spoke well of him.

"Bad report"—other people slandered him.

"Genuine"—some people saw him as sincere.

"Regarded as imposters"—many saw Paul and his crew as counterfeits.

"Known"—many people knew and followed Paul.

"regarded as unknown"—some people saw him as a nobody and encouraged people not to follow him.

"Dying"—Paul risked death often.

"We live on"—Paul knew he was living under resurrection power.

"Beaten"—Paul had many setbacks, and many saw him as finished.

"Not killed"—no physical problems could finish Paul.

"Sorrowful"—Paul knew what it was to mourn.

"Always rejoicing"—in Christ, Paul still had joy.

"Poor"—Paul was not in the ministry to get rich.

"Making many rich"—Paul was in the ministry to help others.

"Having nothing"—materially, Paul looked broke.

"Possessing everything"—Paul knew his inheritance in Christ was sure.

In spite of all of the difficulties, Paul remained open to the people for whom he ministered. He was open to the very ones who were closed to him. And he moved to discuss that in the next section.

Our Partnerships (6:11—7:1)

One of the ways in which we can receive God's grace in vain is by maintaining wrong partnerships. Of course, the opposite of wrong partnerships is correct partnerships. In this next section, Paul deals with what partnerships Christians should have and what partnerships they should not have.

Correct Partnerships (11-13)

When Paul said, "We have spoken freely to you," he was referring to the fact that he never had hidden agendas with them. That is one mark of a functioning partner. He had room in his heart for them. "We . . . opened wide our hearts to you." That means that he did not withhold his affection from them. In doing that, he did not pay back to them what they were doing to him. In fact, they did withhold their love toward him. Now Paul asked them to reciprocate by sharing their partnership, their affection, their fellowship with him.

Christians will not be able to be effective people helpers to others if they are not willing to help one another. Jesus got at that when He said, "All men will know that you are my disciples, if you love another" (John 13:35).

When Paul spoke about both his mouth and his heart, he was making it clear that he didn't have just a "mouthy" ministry. His ministry had heart to it! The use of his mouth was to say that he was carrying out effectively the "*message* of reconciliation" (2 Corinthians 5:19). When he spoke about his open heart, he made it clear that he was also carrying out responsibly his "*ministry* of reconciliation" (2 Corinthians 5:18). Jesus used the term *hypocrites* to describe people who had a lip religion without a love tied to it (Matthew 15:8).

A death blow to any congregation is accepting the attitude seen in the words, "But you are withholding yours from us." Paul said literally, "You are restrained in your own affections." While Paul's affections were wide, theirs were narrow. Paul's was wide to include them, but theirs were narrow to exclude him.

Anytime church members manifest a restrictive affection towards one another by being overly critical, overly suspicious, neglectful, and insensitive to one another, then the beginning of the death blow of that congregation has started. Paul knew what it meant to be closed out of the hearts of his brothers and sisters, and sadly, many Christians today also feel that.

While Paul called for the Corinthians to widen their hearts, it is possible to have our hearts too wide. And that is what Paul moved to in the next paragraph.

Incorrect Partnerships (6:14 − 7:1)

Another way to receive the grace of God in vain is to have wrong partnerships that affect our life-styles. And that is Paul's point in this section.

Just what did Paul mean when he said, "Do not be yoked together with unbelievers"? Here are some possible options:
1. Do not be involved in mixed marriages (a Christian with a non-Christian).
2. Isolate yourself from pagan people.
3. Do not be involved in pagan practices—thus being a functioning partner with non-believers.

Although it is popular to suggest that Paul was talking against mixed marriages, that seems unlikely in this context. While Christians can make a case against mixed marriages, using this section as a prooftext that commands against it presents some problems. Here are some reasons for thinking that Paul was not speaking against mixed marriages as his primary subject:

1. Paul had not been discussing the topic of marriage in the immediate context, nor did he discuss that topic anywhere in this chapter.

2. Paul already discussed the topic of mixed marriages in 1 Corinthians 7:12, and in that chapter he did not suggest that a believer should separate from his married partner who was a non-believer. In fact, he made it clear that the believer should remain with the non-believer in a marriage relationship. How does that advice square with what we read here, if Paul here was talking about mixed marriages also? How could Paul have encouraged the believer to stay married if a believer can have no fellowship with a non-believer in a marriage, can have nothing in common with the non-Christian in a marriage, can have no agreement with the non-Christian, must be separate from them, and cannot touch them?

3. Peter certainly did not understand 2 Corinthians 6:14—7:1 to be speaking of being married to an unbeliever, for Peter gave clear instructions about how a believing wife should live with an unbelieving husband (1 Peter 3:1-6).

4. The immediate context of 2 Corinthians suggests that Paul was developing the fact that a Christian should not cave in to, adopt, or become a sharing partner in, the pagan life-style of those around him with whom he does associate.

5. The verse immediately following 2 Corinthians 6:18 gives a strong indication that Paul was not really referring to a marital situation primarily. The next verse is 2 Corinthians 7:1, which begins with the word *since*. The word *since* always introduces a reason for saying the preceding words. In chapter 7:1, Paul talked about "these promises." The promises Paul referred to are the promises of God to receive us and to be our Father. There is nothing in the entire New Testament that suggests that God will not receive us or be our Father if we are married to a non-Christian. However, a person who is a participant in a pagan life-style simply has little room in his heart for apostolic teaching, for repentance, or for having a heart open wide to Christian

teachers and preachers. A person who is participating in a pagan life-style is not open to being involved in a message of reconciliation or a ministry of reconciliation. That person has forgotten that the old has passed away and the new has come. That person has forgotten that he is now living in Christ and has taken on the new righteousness of which Paul spoke in the preceding chapter.

Evidently some of the Corinthians took Paul's teaching in 1 Corinthians 5:9-11 too far. In those verses, Paul encouraged the Corinthians to associate with the non-Christians in their communities. Some, however, did not just associate with non-Christian people, but also participated in non-Christian practices, and that is what Paul was condemning in this section. Some may have even gone so far as to participate in the non-Christian worship services, thus a reference to idols (2 Corinthians 6:16).

Nor does this section mean that the Christian should remain isolated from pagan people. That cannot stand when we look at Jesus' example. The church is to be light, salt, and leaven. The church cannot be that if it does not have any touching relationships with non-Christians. Jesus made it clear that He was like a physician who came for the sick.

In 2 Corinthians 6:14, Paul literally said, "Stop becoming yoked together." So he was not suggesting that they stop marrying non-Christians, for they had already done that, but rather that they stop being participants with their non-Christian friends. He didn't tell them not to associate, but rather to be cautious, to keep boundaries drawn in those associations. There is a degree of friendliness with the world that is at odds with God (James 4:4).

The words *yoked together* refer to two people being so connected in partnership that the methods, priorities, and strategies of one become the other's. The reasons are many, as follows:

1. Righteousness and wickedness do not have anything in common.

2. The term *in common* is the Greek word for fellowship that is based upon external things. It is a word that describes people who are in partnership with a similar goal in mind. What has bound them together is not anything that has connected them internally, but rather externally—like a business, like an investment, like a project.

3. There is no fellowship between light and darkness. The word *fellowship* is a Greek word that refers to being linked together

internally. There is certainly no internal linkage because of the contrast that we see in this chapter. Just look at those contrasts:

Righteousness	Wickedness
Light	Darkness
Christ	Belial
Believer	Unbeliever
Temple of God	Idols

4. There is no "harmony." The word *harmony* is from a Greek word from which we get the word *symphony*. A symphony refers to an "agreement." Instruments are blending together with one another. It is a concert of mutuality that requires total cooperation with one another. *Belial* is a term that was recognized in the first century as one of the names for Satan. It literally means worthlessness.

5. The believer does not have anything "in common" with an unbeliever. The words *in common* come from a Greek word that Paul used in 1 Corinthians 12 to refer to the fact that Christians are members of one another. We are "a part" of one another. In fact, the Greek word literally means to be "a part." It was used to describe parts of a physical body that belong to one another, were to be supportive of one another, and were united to one another, because they were indeed united with one another. To the degree that a believer begins to identify himself as a member of the unbeliever, then the believer's heart is far too wide. He indeed will be restricted from doing the "one another's" for his brothers and sisters in Christ. The Christian who does not understand who his real brothers and sisters in Christ are is a person who is confused about his eternal identity.

6. There is no agreement between the temple of God and idols. The word *agreement* literally means to "place down with." It is a phrase that refers to partnership. It was used for putting down votes together. One person puts his vote down and the other person puts his vote down in total agreement with the first person. They join together in their project.

It is God who lives inside the Christian and walks among the Christians. Christians are to be God's people (2 Corinthians

6:16). Therefore, we are to come out from them and be separate. But that does not mean to come out from association with people, for the gospel must touch people. It does mean to come out from partnership with the practices of those people. When Paul said, "Touch no unclean thing" (2 Corinthians 6:17), he was referring to the unclean practices. Some of the Corinthian Christians had evidently been captivated by those practices, as are several Christians today.

The words *be separate* refer to the idea of marking off boundaries beyond which we are not to go. Christians are not to form any partnership with non-Christians that would involve a compromise of practices. While we may think it is impossible to function in the world without that, God promises that He will be a Father to us—and that means He will be the supply source for our strength, energy, and survival.

Paul concluded this section with a call for us to have a proper relationship with both deeds and deity. We are to have a proper relationship with deeds: "Let us purify ourselves from everything that contaminates body and spirit." We are to have a proper relationship by God: "... perfecting holiness out of reverence for God" (2 Corinthians 7:1).

What does it mean to perfect holiness? The word *holy* refers to being set apart for God. But that does not mean we separate ourselves from people. In fact, quite the contrary. To be set apart from God is to be set apart for God's priorities and purposes with His character. It is to commit ourselves to what He is committed to. In fact, the word for *holy* was used in the first century for a marriage situation. When two people got married, they were "set apart" for each other. Part of that "setting apart" meant that each person was to be committed to the priorities of the other person. Each was to seek to make the other successful. Consequently our "holiness out of reverence for God" is to seek to make God successful in what He is trying to do on planet earth. And what God is trying to do is to reconcile all mankind to himself. That, then, requires that His people touch non-Christians, speak with non-Christians, and be in a ministry of reconciliation with non-Christians as well as with Christians.

The word *perfecting* is a Greek word that means to make complete or mature. Our being committed to God reaches maturity when we involve ourselves with people the way Jesus did. No one had more mature holiness (a setting apart to, a commitment for

God) than Jesus. But Jesus refused to adopt the Pharisaic attitude of being separated from the "untouchables." He was known as a friend of the sinners. He spent time with socially unfit. He allowed some of the most "undesirables" to minister to Him. Various kinds of people who had been left out by the religious institution felt drawn in to Jesus by His friendships. But while Jesus did that, He never caved in to the daily life-style of those with whom He became friends. He remained cleansed from anything that could contaminate His body and Spirit. At the same time, He remained open to the people whom God loved. That is the way Jesus purified himself on the one hand and on the other hand perfected holiness out of reverence for God. And that's precisely what He modeled for His disciples. And out of that modeling, He gave them the invitation, "Follow Me." And that is His challenge to each of us still.

Do we want to "purify ourselves from everything that contaminates body and spirit"? Then we must flee from the non-Christlike activities that non-Christian friends may be engaged in and may encourage us to do also. Do we want to be involved in "perfecting holiness out of reverence for God"? Then we must reach out to the kinds of people for whom Jesus came and with whom Jesus associated—the kinds of people that right now feel left out from institutionalized religion. And we must do that out of reverence for God, for we stand in awe of His purpose that He set in motion in Genesis 3 and that He brought to reality in the coming of Jesus.

While our hearts are to be opened wide to have affection for the non-believers, our ethics are to be narrow so we don't include their ethics.

If we do not understand Paul's advice in this passage to refer to mixed marriages, does that open the gate for any Christian to marry a non-Christian? Of course not! But it does say that Paul is not contradicting his advice to those who were in marriages in 1 Corinthians 7. There he made it clear that there is to be a separation, but it is not a separation from the marriage relationship, but a separation from the participating partnership in any relationship in which Christians are caving in to the life-style of the pagans.

Here are some practical reasons why the Christian should be extremely cautious in marrying a non-Christian—and, in fact, should not do so:

1. Our Father wants married life to be lived out in peace (1 Corinthians 7:15). A Christian marrying a non-Christian can get himself into a very tension-filled and frustrating situation that builds animosities. Of course, this depends upon the nature, makeup, and priorities of both of those people.

2. The non-Christian may not accept, appreciate, approve, or in any way want to reflect any of the life-style of the Christian mate. When this happens, then the happiness level and the partnership level of the Christian and non-Christian can widen. As a matter of fact, the non-Christian may decide that he or she does not want to be a part of someone who has a life-style that is so diametrically opposed to the pagan's. That may cause the non-Christian mate to get out of the marital relationship. That is permissible by 1 Corinthians 7, but that can add a great deal of trauma for the Christian mate.

3. Often, the Christian may have to make decisions that are tremendously uncomfortable for him or her to make in a mixed marriage.

4. A Christian who loves the church and the activities of the church wants to give time, energy, and money to the program of the church. But he or she may be prevented from doing that or may be reluctant to do so in an effort not to create unnecessary tension with his or her mate. Thus, having a more meaningful and fulfilled life as a Christian may be stifled in a mixed marriage.

5. God expects a husband and wife to cleave to each other. That is a strong Hebrew word that means that nothing is to come between the two. It is quite possible that the relationship between the two could emerge in such a way that the church comes between the two people who are married. Of course, this does not happen in every mixed marriage, because there are some unbelieving mates who understand, appreciate, encourage, and enhance the Christian's activity in the Lord's work. But when a mate is not that way, then the church, God, and Jesus Christ can come between the cleaving of the husband and the wife. In fact, Jesus makes it clear that this will happen (Matthew 10).

6. The real issue, however, is that the Christian's potential contribution to other people around him for the Lord's name's sake and the use of that Christian's gifts within and for the family of God are certainly dampened, thwarted, and sometimes undeveloped because of the lack of encouragement from the un-Christian partner.

7. The Christian who is married to a non-Christian often finds that he or she is unable to share the experiences, the emotions, and the dreams with the mate that inside he or she so desperately wants to share. They often do not share worship experiences together. They often do not share reading the Bible together. They often do not share praying together. They often do not share going to Christian activities and participating in services together. That can bring a bit of emptiness and deep loneliness into the life of the Christian mate who desperately wants to share this important aspect of his or her life with the mate.

So while there is little evidence that Paul was dealing with mixed marriages in 2 Corinthians 6:14—7:1, that does not mean that Paul would have encouraged such practice. Instead of dealing with mixed marriages, Paul was dealing with a situation that was preventing the Corinthians from having a heart wide open to him, preventing them from being involved in the ministry of reconciliation to which God has called them, preventing them from accepting the new life, preventing them from enjoying what it meant to be a new creation. That is the immediate context of this passage. It could include a mixed marriage, but it is not restricted to it.

At no time in history is caution more needed than today when we all live in the midst of such a pluralistic society with both Christians and non-Christians touching bases at nearly every experience. Christians are to be light in the midst of that, but are not to cave in to it.

Summary

1. Christians can receive the grace of God in vain.

2. Receiving the grace of God in vain means that we do not take on the responsibilities of being servants of reconciliation for others.

3. *In vain* means worthless; so we are not fulfilling our potential with our gifts that God has given to us for others.

4. Christians are to live out their purpose with God's privileges in a way that does not put a stumbling block in front of others. That refers both to our conduct and to how we react in difficult situations.

5. Christians are not immune to difficult times, but we are to react to them with Christlikeness.

6. Christians are to be engaged in a functioning partnership with other Christians.

7. Christians are to refrain from adopting the life-style of non-Christians with whom they associate.

8. Perfecting holiness is continuing to be set apart to God by committing ourselves to live for His priorities and purposes and with His character. God's priorities and purpose are for people. He loves people and expects us to reach out to meet their needs.

CHAPTER SEVEN

The Joys of a People Helper

2 Corinthians 7:2-16

While at one time, Paul was in the pits, "We were under great pressure, far beyond our ability to endure, so that we despaired even of life" (2 Corinthians 1:8), Paul here talked about being on the mountaintop. This chapter is filled with the joys of a people helper. Just look at the joyful terms that Paul scattered throughout this brief chapter (2 Corinthians 7):

   Great confidence (verse 4)
   Great pride (verse 4)
   Greatly encouraged (verse 4)
   Joy knows no bounds (verse 4)
   Comfort (verses 6, 7)
   Joy was greater than ever (verse 7)
   Am happy (verse 9)
   Delighted (verse 13)
   Happy (verse 13)
   Boasted (verse 14)
   Boasting (verse 14)
   Affection is all the greater (verse 15)
   I am glad (verse 16)
   Complete confidence (verse 16)

What is it that brings such joyful response in a people helper? It is the evidence that the people were really helped. It is the evidence that people have taken seriously the outreach from the people helper. It is to note change in people toward godliness. The greatest joys of people helpers are not the days they pick up their paychecks, but rather the times they see that their investment in people has not been in vain, but rather is returning wonderful dividends in the lives of those people.

A Confident Appeal for Mutual Love (7:2-4)

Paul repeated his appeal that he gave in 2 Corinthians 6:13: "Open wide your hearts." Here he repeated it with confidence, a confidence generated by the report from Titus that the Corinthians were really interested in changing. Even though Paul was giving instructions for a major change they would yet have to go through in order to open wide their affection for him, he was confident they would do it. He had just finished outlining that major change above. Their widening affection for him would partly depend upon their decision not to participate in the lifestyle of their unbelieving acquaintances. But Paul was confident that the Corinthians would follow his instructions because of the report that Titus had brought.

Paul's confidence is seen in the words, "I have great confidence in you; I take great pride in you. I am greatly encouraged; in all our troubles my joy knows no bounds" (2 Corinthians 7:4). In the two verses just before that, Paul may have been answering some charges that were still lingering in Corinth, which Titus could have reported to him. When Paul said, "We have wronged no one," he literally said that he had treated no one unjustly. It may be that some had suggested to Titus that Paul's stern letter (2 Corinthians 2:3, 4) was too harsh—unjust.

There are several activities of a people helper that are spotlighted in these three verses:

1. Treat no one unjustly.

2. Corrupt no one, either by a bad example in life-style or by teaching.

3. Do not take advantage of anyone: "We have exploited no one" (2 Corinthians 7:2).

4. Do not keep score of wrongs done to you. This is spotlighted by Paul's words, "I do not say this to condemn you" (2 Corinthians 7:3). Paul did not have any revenge toward them for the charges that some of them were making against him. He did not speak to them with hostility. That itself is a mark of maturity.

5. Show the depth of commitment to the people you help. Paul did that when he said, "We would live or die with you" (2 Corinthians 7:3).

6. Show confidence in people: "I have great confidence in you" (2 Corinthians 7:4). People want to live up to the confidence they know that other people have in them. It is great to be trusted. A person does not have to improve much if he feels people do not

have confidence in him. Having confidence in people is one of the finest ways to express being a real people helper.

7. Take pride in people, "I take great pride in you" (2 Corinthians 7:4). Paul elsewhere wrote, "Honor one another above yourselves" (Romans 12:10). Paul knew how to praise people even though he had disciplined them. He even praised them to Titus before Titus journeyed toward them. That caused Titus to approach them with a positive attitude. We do not help people by cutting them down, belittling them, and showing lack of respect for them. Every parent who has raised children understands the great positive motivation of showing a bit of pride in the worth and potential and activities of people.

8. Express encouragement in others, "I am greatly encouraged" (2 Corinthians 7:4). People need a shot of positive reinforcement.

9. Express joy, "In all our troubles my joy knows no bounds" (2 Corinthians 7:4). People need optimism, not pessimism. People need to see others who are buoyed up even amid their troubles.

All of the above shows the part of positive thinking and positive living that God expects from people helpers. When a person manifests these kinds of qualities, then the people he is trying to help do not have to go into a self-defensive mode. They do not have to justify themselves at the expense of others. They do not have to fight back. It is difficult to lash out and fight back at someone who is not treating you unjustly or is not exploiting you, someone who is willing to stick with you through thick and thin (live or die with you), or someone who has confidence in you, has pride in you, is encouraged about you, and manifests joy in your presence. Those are essential qualities for effective people management.

Specifics for Paul's Joy (7:5-16)

After Paul said he was greatly encouraged and that his joy knew no bounds, he then moved to discuss briefly the various specifics that were giving him that boundless joy. Those specifics are scattered throughout the rest of this chapter.

The Meeting With Titus (5-7)

This section picks up where Paul left off in 2 Corinthians 2:13. Remember, he had arranged to meet Titus in Troas to discover how things were going with the Corinthian church. However, when Titus was not in Troas, Paul's uneasiness caused him to

113

journey towards Macedonia in order to see Titus as soon as possible.

This paragraph also begins to explain how Paul was so elated and encouraged. Paul admitted that he was somewhat down when he came into Macedonia. He was physically fatigued. "This body of ours had no rest, but we were harassed at every turn" (2 Corinthians 7:5), and he had both internal and external pressures. The word for *harassed* is the word that pictures the crushing of grain or wheat. Paul was really under pressure. The pressures from "the outside" evidently came from opposition he was receiving from within the Macedonian environment. Macedonia had been a tough area for Paul. His first stay in Macedonia was in Philippi, which resulted in a riot and imprisonment (Acts 16). He next went to Thessalonica, where he evidently was able to stay only three weeks and was ordered out. In fact, at Thessalonica, Christians had to post a bond (Acts 17:9), which was probably their guarantee that Paul would not come back into the city. When Paul then went to Berea, some Jews from Thessalonica followed him and stirred up the crowd to agitation.

As Paul was writing this letter, he had just reentered Macedonia for the first time since those bitter experiences. Consequently, that external environment was a pressure on him, which was coupled with an internal pressure, "fears within." Paul's internal fear probably zeroed in on three things. First was a fear concerning the safety of Titus. Why hadn't Titus showed up in Troas? How had the Corinthians received him? Had he encountered danger in either Corinth or traveling on the road after leaving Corinth? Second were Paul's fears concerning how the Corinthian church received Titus and Paul's earlier letter. And the third fear concerned how the Macedonian people who had so mistreated him before were going to treat him. Every morning, he must have awakened wondering what the day would bring to him. The primary concern, however, seems to have been zeroed in on the safety of Titus and the situation in Corinth.

But God are two power-packed words in the New Testament. It would be interesting to look at every place those words appear in order to see how God makes a difference. While Paul was discomforted in verse 5, he was comforted in verse 6, and the change is seen in the words *but God*.

Ever been downcast? Then shake hands with Paul, for he admitted that he was downcast (2 Corinthians 7:6). Ever experience being humbled uncomfortably? Then shake hands with Paul, for the word *downcast* in the Greek literally means humbled. Paul was humbled by the Corinthians' reaction to him. He was humbled by their rejection. He was humbled by the fact that many did not see him in a good light. Ever experience God's intervening in your life and making a change in those down times? Then shake hands with Paul.

When Paul talked about how God comforted him in this downcast time, he was taking us back to 2 Corinthians 1, where he talked about God's being the God of all comfort. Though God is the source of all comfort, the way that comfort comes is often through people. God specializes in comforting through people. In fact, when people are used by God to comfort others, they are involved in a ministry of reconciliation. So God comforted Paul by protecting Titus on his journeys and by working in the lives of the Corinthians to make a significant change in their situation. Paul picked up on both of these by spotlighting the comfort that came, "by the coming of Titus," and "by the comfort you had given him."

Paul was not a Lone Ranger Christian. He thrived in working in relationships with others. Seldom did he work alone, and seldom was he apart from the fellowship and encouragement and the help of his brothers and sisters in a team ministry. Being lonely can feed the feeling of being downcast. Paul rejoiced when people came to him. He mentioned that in 1 Corinthians 16:17, "I was glad when Stephanas, Fortunatus and Achaicus arrived." When God brought healing to Epaphroditus that enabled him to remain with Paul, Paul said that prevented him from having sorrow upon sorrow (Philippians 2:27).

When Paul was alone in prison, he wrote to Timothy and said, "Do your best to come to me quickly" (2 Timothy 4:9). There is strength in fellowship. There is encouragement in fellowship. There is joy in fellowship. So Paul's downer became an upper when Titus arrived. Do you know someone in the midst of a downer now? Part of your ministry of reconciliation could be a telephone call, a telegram, or better yet, a personal visit.

Just the coming of Titus brought comfort to Paul. But also the positive attitude Titus held brought comfort to Paul. Optimism spreads. Titus couldn't wait to share with Paul three truths about the Corinthians' situation. And each of these truths had to do with the Corinthians' relationship with Paul:

1. A longing for Paul.
2. A deep sorrow on the part of the Corinthians.
3. An ardent concern for Paul.

The Corinthians wanted to see Paul. They had a deep sorrow for their carnality, which fed their feelings of alienation against Paul, and they had a concern for Paul's concern. They had an anxiety about Paul's anxiety. They had a concern about the pressures Paul was going through, much of which was caused by the Corinthians' criticism and their obstinance to change.

But notice that Paul was not just comforted by the fact that the Corinthians were now open to him, but also was comforted by Titus's comfort. There is a tremendous significance to body life in the church. The joy of one person spreads to others. The sorrow of one person spreads to others. The optimism of one person spreads to others. The pessimism of one person spreads to others. And the comfort of one person spreads to others.

The comfort that Titus experienced touched Paul and gave him comfort. That kind of touching is a way to be a people helper. Titus was a people helper for Paul. But that kind of positive spread cannot happen unless we touch bases with one another. And when we touch bases with one another, we need to be open to let them know what is going on in our lives.

After Titus touched Paul in fellowship and with a positive optimistic attitude, Paul said, "My joy was greater than ever" (2 Corinthians 7:7). One of the ways to be a people helper and thus to be involved in a ministry of reconciliation is to help lift up other people. Real Christian love is the desire to want the other person's joy to be "greater than ever."

The Change in the Corinthians (8-12)

Paul's joy was not that people had been humiliated and hurt (2 Corinthians 7:8), but rather that the people to whom he had written his letter had been helped (2 Corinthians 7:9).

Paul admitted that he had had a temporary regret over his painful letter that he mentioned in 2 Corinthians 2:3, 4. While some people delight in having the kind of power that can hurt others, Paul did not. Their hurt affected him. That's the kind of oneness he felt with them. He actually felt firsthand their feelings. He had true empathy. Paul personally lived out what he said, "If one part suffers, every part suffers with it; if one part is honored, every part rejoices with it" (1 Corinthians 12:26).

Evidently, Paul's letter did bring them grief for a while, "You were made sorry." Evidently, their initial grief came without producing change, and that caused Paul some regret. But their grief eventually led them to repentance, and that brought Paul joy (2 Corinthians 7:8, 9).

When a person faces his wrongs honestly and realizes those wrongs have hurt himself and others, there is initial grief. Grief is positive, for it lets us know that something has gone wrong. But people can do different things with their grief. They can allow their grief to put them into the pits where they stay the rest of their lives in depression. It can cause them to rationalize what they have done for self-justification. Then the grief leads to no change. Or it can cause them to face squarely the cause of that grief and then to make changes in their lives. That is repentance. And that is what happened with the church at Corinth.

But notice, it did not happen immediately. We should never give up on a person who is going through difficult times. Paul had written several letters, made visits, and sent other people to the Corinthian situation before repentance finally broke out. The Greek word for *repentance* comes from two words that mean "after" and "thought." Thus, it comes after a person has had time to think about the situation. Repentance involves several aspects:

1. A knowing—sin is recognized.
2. A feeling—sin is disliked.
3. A willingness—sin is disowned.

However, none of the three above, by itself, is repentance. For just recognition of sin may make a person defiant or move him into rationalization. Just a sorrow over sin my lead him to despair and even suicide. Just the abandonment of sin alone may be due to just wisdom (the wise and safe thing to do), or for social or security reasons (in order to keep a job or be seen in a good light), and not because sin is hated and disowned. So all three of the above must work together.

Real repentance always involves a reorientation of one's life. It is not enough just to forsake sin. One must also adopt a new ethical code. The inward action is to be seen by the corresponding outer action. Real repentance is both a turn *from* and a turn *to*. It involves both an abandonment and an acceptance—that is, an abandonment of the old ways and an acceptance of the new way.

Faith, repentance, and baptism go together. Without faith, there is no repentance. Without repentance, there is no saving faith. And faith and repentance lead to baptism. Faith and repentance are necessary for a death to self, and baptism is a visible burial of that self.

Baptism is an outward demonstration of what has been going on inwardly. Faith changes a person's perspective, repentance changes a person's practices, and baptism changes a person's position. For a person who is baptized puts on Christ (Galatians 3:27). And in Christ a person becomes a new creation (2 Corinthians 5:17).

Before the recognition of sin leads one to repentance, there must be a sorrow for that sin. Paul said, "Your sorrow led you to repentance" (2 Corinthians 7:9). There are two kinds of sorrow: godly sorrow and worldly sorrow. Let's look at the two of them.

Godly sorrow. The Greek construction really says, "grief according to God." It is the kind of grief that God has, and it is the kind of grief God wants. It is not just a grief where a person has been caught in his sin, but a genuine sorrow over the wrong that the sin has done, not only to oneself, but also to God and to others. Godly sorrow involves a grief over the hurt that the offense has produced. That kind of grief motivates a person to repentance. For that kind of person sees sin for what it really is and then takes responsibility for it. Only then can a real reorientation result.

Worldly sorrow. Worldly sorrow involves having a real sorrow, but it is a selfish sorrow. It is a remorse over being caught and the consequences that will come to oneself. It can involve a guilt, but won't accept responsibility for it. Worldly grief blames everyone else for the sin—the environment, parents, the friends, the devil, or anyone. Worldly sorrow is a grief over the loss of face because other people know about the error. Worldly sorrow is not really concerned about the wrong done. Worldly sorrow can lead to death. It can lead to death in the following ways:

1. Emotional death. That happens when a person goes through self-torture and can find no way out.

2. A spiritual death. The person may be sorry that he has been caught but not sorry for his sin. Thus, he may plan to do the same kind of things in more deceitful ways so that he does not get caught again. Then the person goes further into spiritual depravity.

3. Social death. In this case, the person isolates himself from others out of guilt.

4. Physical death. Anytime a person is overwhelmed with grief and does not work out of it, there are unhealthy reactions that go on inside of a person's body. The physical death can also include actual suicide due to the depression.

5. Sensitivity death. A person who has initial worldly sorrow over his sin but does not move to reorient himself out of that sin can eventually become insensitive to that sin. He can stay in it so long that he becomes hardhearted and is no longer even affected by exposure. That can lead him to more serious, open offenses. It can cause him not to care who knows or who is hurt or offended. A person who has hurt someone else and only has grief because he has been caught will not be moved to change. Instead, he may eventually be moved to murder.

All of the above kinds of worldly sorrow bring loss to the person. It brings separation—separation from God, separation from self, separation from others, and separation from joy. That's death. But godly sorrow that leads to repentance has benefits that cannot be lost.

1. Psychological benefits. The person who repents can come to the place of accepting himself.

2. Sociological benefits. The person who repents does not have to keep himself isolated from his peers. His shame is removed.

3. Physical benefits. The person who repents reverses the disease that comes through worldly sorrow and guilt.

4. Spiritual benefits. The person who repents is reconciled both to God and to his fellowman.

Consequently, repentance is necessary both for loving God and for loving others as we love ourselves. Repentance is not just an act over one's own situation. It is an attitude and activity about one's whole style of life. Repentance helps a person to turn from selfishness to selflessness.

There are several products that come out of genuine repentance. Paul mentions them in 2 Corinthians 7:10, 11.

1. Salvation. The word *salvation* deals with wholeness. Repentance brings a person to total wholeness. Repentance is very therapeutic.

2. Earnestness. That means that the Corinthians no longer had a careless indifference toward sin. They got thoroughly busy in being earnest.

3. Eagerness to clear oneself. The Greek word for *eagerness* literally means defense. But it doesn't refer to someone's going into self-defense by making excuses, but rather to clear themselves by reconciling the wrong. They needed to "clear" the bad reputation the church was having by correcting the situation and by changing their own perspectives.

4. Indignation. That is an inner wrath, not just over the sin, but also over the scandal that the sin and the people's reactions to that sin had brought to the church.

5. Alarm. That refers to being alarmed over possible judgment if they would not change. It was alarm over God's displeasure, alarm over the way that sin has hurt themselves, others, God, and the reputation of the church. That can also include an alarm over whether or not they had done all they needed to do in changing.

6. Longing. That would refer to a longing for God's pleasure, a longing to change, a longing to be more effective, a longing for Paul to come to visit the Corinthians, a longing for reconciliation with themselves, with others, with the apostle, and with God.

7. Concern. This is really the Greek word for zeal. It is to be enthusiastic for pleasing God and leaving nothing undone that they might do prior to Paul's arrival.

8. A readiness to see justice done. This is from a Greek word that means to make something right. The Corinthians had been understanding justice as only punishment for the man who had sinned in 1 Corinthians 5. But justice also involves acquittal. It involves forgiveness. It involves a clearing. The Corinthians had not received the man back after he had repented, but evidently after Titus' visit, they had done so.

Because the Corinthians had gone through all of the above, Paul said in an encouraging word, "At every point you have proved yourselves to be innocent in this matter" (2 Corinthians 7:11). How could they be innocent when they were guilty? That is because when God forgives, He cleans the slate. And when God forgives, He forgets about the sin entirely. A person for whom God cannot remember a sin is a person who is innocent in the sight of God. And he is even innocent in himself, for God removes that sin. If a person continues to have guilt, then it is self-imposed guilt and has no rightful place in the life of a forgiven person. The words *at every point* might not just refer to the above ways they had changed, but could refer to "every point" in which they had sinned. At every sin, at every reaction, at every mistake,

God had forgiven them because of their repentance. What a beautiful description of the breadth and inclusiveness of God's forgiveness to the Christian who sins.

Some people feel that God will forgive a non-Christian when he becomes a Christian, but that He does not eagerly forgive people after they become Christians. That is heresy. God's forgiveness for a Christian within the family of God is as inclusive (all sins), available, and effective as for the non-Christian when he is reconciled in Christ.

Because they had changed, they could surely understand the motive behind Paul's painful letter to them. He wrote out of love for them, because he knew the seriousness to their lives if they did not change. He did not write to them in order to get back at them in a negative way or to stick up for certain people who were being mistreated by the Corinthians. He wasn't taking sides when he wrote to them about his pain. The only side that he was taking was God's side—love for the whole church at Corinth.

Titus's Reaction (13-16)

The positive reaction of a Christian is contagious. Encouragement is contagious (2 Corinthians 7:13). A positive outlook is contagious (2 Corinthians 7:14). Affection is contagious (2 Corinthians 7:15). Joy and confidence are contagious (2 Corinthians 7:16).

When Paul saw that Titus was refreshed, that delighted Paul. But notice something interesting in this closing paragraph. Paul had sent Titus to Corinth with a positive attitude about Corinth. He could have bad-mouthed Corinth in front of Titus so much that Titus would have gone in with a negative attitude, not expecting a positive response. Titus could have approached the Corinthians with harshness, with suspicion, and with lack of confidence in their reception. But Paul boasted about the Corinthians to Titus. So when he arrived in Corinth, he arrived with possibility thinking. Paul's big heart (2 Corinthians 6:13; 7:3) is seen by the fact that in spite of all the difficulties the Corinthians were giving to Paul, Paul built the Corinthians up in Titus's hearing. That gave Titus affection for the Corinthians before he ever got there. Titus arrived in Corinth with loving, not with loathing, and that love increased after he got there, and it continued to increase after he left.

Not only did Paul build up the Corinthians to Titus, but here he built up the Corinthians to themselves by saying, "You have not embarrassed me," and, "As everything we said to you was true, so our boasting about you to Titus has proved to be true as well," and, "I am glad I can have complete confidence in you" (2 Corinthians 7:14-16). What a beautiful attitude of a people helper to people who need help. What a beautiful attitude of a people helper to people who have purposely hurt that people helper! What a beautiful attitude of being a minister of reconciliation and sharing a message of reconciliation!

Summary

1. We need to spend time building people up and not tearing them down.

2. The optimistic positive attitudes of one Christian can affect others.

3. God comforts the downcast through people who touch their lives.

4. The joy of a people helper is in the people he helps.

5. A people helper should help others in sin to come to the place of godly sorrow.

6. Worldly sorrow brings loss.

7. Godly sorrow brings benefits because it leads to repentance.

8. What every person has done can be forgiven.

9. A person may more likely change if we tell his good points to a people helper and not poison the mind of a people helper with the negative things about the person he wants to help.

10. We need to build up people with positive stroking and encouraging remarks, both about them to others and about them to themselves.

CHAPTER EIGHT

Motivations for Helping People With Our Money

2 Corinthians 8

Introduction

The test of some Christians is seen in the reaction that comes when the topic turns from being Christlike with our morals to being Christlike with our money. Each of us needs to evaluate why we bristle a bit when Christian leaders ask for our generosity in giving. Does one of the following affect us?

1. We evaluate our worth by the money we have.
2. We evaluate our security by the money we have.
3. We evaluate our success by the money we have.
4. We evaluate our power by the money we have.
5. We evaluate our status by the money we have.
6. We evaluate the worth of others by the money they have.

Too often, our goal seems to be to accumulate more money and things money can provide. Thus, to give away those things for the benefit of some other people thwarts reaching our goal. To let go of very much of our money is to threaten our identity, security, success, status, and sense of worth and power.

Paul made it clear in 2 Corinthians 8 and 9 that our use of money to help people is a test of the sincerity of our love. It evaluates our real appreciation for the grace God has given to us.

These two chapters demonstrate that our willingness to be generous is significant to the life of the church in several ways. These significances are often overlooked when we study 2 Corinthians, but I want to point out at least two of them: the significance to fellowship and unity, and the significance to stewardship programs.

The Significance of Generosity to Fellowship and Unity

Giving to another tightens the fellowship and unity between the two. In this case, the givers were primarily Gentiles while the receivers were primarily Jews, for the collection was for the relief of famine victims in Judea. It is true that the church in Jerusalem provided the impetus for worldwide evangelism on the Day of Pentecost; so in a sense, the Gentiles had shared in the spiritual things of the Jerusalem church. Now the Gentiles had an indebtedness to share material things with the Jerusalem church since that need had arisen (Romans 15:25-27).

But the bridge between Jewish and Gentile Christians had not always been a smooth bridge. Some of the Jewish Christians in Jerusalem gave strong opposition against Gentile Christians being in the church (see Acts 15), and some Macedonian Gentile Christians were anti-Jewish prior to becoming Christians (see Acts 16:20). Perhaps a bit of anti-Jewish sentiment was one reason why there were not enough Jewish families in the city of Philippi for a synagogue. And all that was required to establish a synagogue was the presence of ten Jewish men. So a sense of unity and fellowship between Gentile and Jewish Christians was certainly not universal.

So this act of Gentile Christians' sharing material things for the well-being of their Jewish Christian brothers was an act that could help tighten up the fellowship between the two. The willingness of the Gentiles to give to their Jewish Christian brothers and sisters demonstrated a sense of corporate oneness with them. According to Paul, the wall between the Jews and the Gentiles had been removed in Christ (Ephesians 2:11-22; Galatians 3:28, 29).

Gentile Christians and Jewish Christians were fellow heirs in the family of God. If they were fellow heirs of all God had, then they needed to be willing to share some of that while here on earth.

The Christian family worldwide still has fellowship gaps. The gaps may be between the upper and lower classes, between blacks and whites, between rural and urban people, or between any distinction we might want to draw. But we must grow to the place where those differences no longer make a difference, and we must be sensitive to the needs of another congregation.

The Significance of Generosity to Stewardship Programs

Although 2 Corinthians 8 and 9 are used often to enhance the members' giving, they are usually used out of context. The giving principles in these two chapters were first applied to a giving that was totally earmarked for someone else. It was not giving for in-house bills such as keeping up buildings or providing salaries.

Those costs for the church are essential, but the stewardship of the church must go far beyond just maintaining the local programs.

These two chapters really spotlight giving in order to aid the poor. It is benevolent giving. Some churches do not earmark much for benevolence. In fact, many feel that giving to relieve physical discomfort is too non-spiritual and temporary. However, Paul devoted time and energy to traveling around the churches for the purpose of collecting a benevolent offering for a famine situation. Surely we can learn from this that God loves the whole person, not just the spiritual side. And surely we can learn that God wants us to walk in His sandals by reaching out to relieve the physical discomforts of people. Stewardship programs of the church must include benevolent giving—especially if those churches continue to use 2 Corinthians 8 and 9 as motivational principles for stewardship programs. Poverty was common in the first century and the first-century church took the responsibility to help relieve poverty seriously (Acts 2:44, 45: 4:32-37).

Paul was concerned about this level of giving early in his ministry (Galatians 2:9, 10). And James makes it clear that Christians who do not take seriously the sharing to relieve another person's physical needs practice a sham Christianity (James 2:1-17).

Christians today, as then, need to be motivated to share their material provisions with others who have need. In this chapter, Paul spotlighted several examples to help prod that motivation.

1. The example of another church (2 Corinthians 8:1-5). Thus church giving reports can be helpful. Sometimes we may think that a church should never report any of the statistics to anyone, lest that be bragging, but statistical reports can be a motivational factor for other congregations.

2. The history of the local congregation's giving (2 Corinthians 8:6, 7). It can be important to consider the past activities of a congregation. History can be helpful if we do not become cemented to it.

3. The example of Jesus (2 Corinthians 8:8, 9). A close study of the Gospels can be tremendously motivational for our unselfishness.

4. The exhortation to "express their impression" (2 Corinthians 8:10-12). As has been observed, "Impression without expression leads to depression." Thus, the making of goals can be helpful as a motivational aid. Some Christians are against any

goal-making when it comes to Christian activities. Their excuse is that if the Holy Spirit is behind it, why should we stifle the Holy Spirit by making goals, but the truth of the matter is that without goals, we stifle the activity of humans. Humans need goals. Humans work with goals. Humans work for goals.

5. The exhortation for equality in needs (2 Corinthians 8:13-15). Thus, a sense of corporate sensitivity is helpful. The stress on fellowship and mutual responsibility is a motivational tool. This is the opposite of a congregation's seeking to live in independence from other congregations.

6. A plan to insure integrity (2 Corinthians 8:16-24). Many people criticize the church's intake of money or they criticize how churches or para-church organizations use the money they receive. It is true that some leaders fly in their private jets and live in the most expensive of life-styles while receiving their money from the Social Security checks of their poor supporters. Consequently, it is significantly important for churches and para-church organizations to design a plan that will communicate integrity in the use of the funds received. Thus, organization and open communication with others is an important motivational tool for encouraging people to share their provisions.

The Motivation of Another Congregation (8:1-5)

While it may at first appear that this chapter is breaking into the context of what Paul had been developing, it really is not. Paul had been spending much time developing the necessity of being a people helper (minister of reconciliation), as well as the character of one who is a people helper.

He spoke about situations in the lives of the Corinthians that had hindered or restricted them from being the kind of people helpers they could have been. But that was beginning to change. The Corinthians had come through repentance and were at this time earnest and eager to do God's work. In fact, they had a readiness to see justice done (2 Corinthians 7:11).

Out of that change, Paul shared his great confidence in them. And here that confidence spilled over into the Corinthians' participating in the collection for the poor saints in Jerusalem. Paul had earlier asked the Corinthians to store up money for that collection (1 Corinthians 16:1-3), and the Corinthians had begun doing that. Apparently, however, they had broken off that activity (2 Corinthians 8:6). Their lack of acceptance of Paul's teaching, their fighting, their division over leadership, their immorality, their greed that caused them to sue one another, their comparison of themselves with each other over spiritual gifts, and their participation in the life-style of their non-Christian friends all contributed to their lack of interest and activity in sharing material goods for their brothers and sisters elsewhere. But here, that had changed.

Prior to the change in the Corinthians' life, Paul could not have brought to their attention the example of another congregation. They would have rebuked that kind of motivation. But they had become open to see how God was using another congregation. So Paul provided that for them by discussing the Macedonian churches.

Paul wrote this from Macedonia. So he had firsthand knowledge and recent data concerning what those congregations were doing about the collection. When Paul talked about the "grace" that God had given to the Macedonian churches, he was not just referring to what God had provided them, but how they were demonstrating that grace in unselfishness. Grace is not just what we receive, but also what we share. Every good work that a Christian does is a result of God's grace. God's grace is in us to be shared. But when we turn our baskets away from other people, then we at the same time turn those baskets away from God for further filling.

Notice how the word *grace* is used in 2 Corinthians 8 and 9.

1. "The grace that God has given the Macedonian churches" (8:1).
2. "This act of grace on your part" (8:6).
3. "This grace of giving" (8:7).
4. "The grace of our Lord Jesus Christ" (8:9).
5. "And God is able to make all grace abound to you" (9:8).
6. "The surpassing grace God has given you" (9:14).

It is clear from the above that in these two chapters, the word *grace* refers either to what God has given to someone else or to what someone else gives away for the benefit of another. To be involved in giving material possessions for the benefit of others is to be involved in a grace work.

The example of the Macedonians is important to notice in many different ways—their source (from God, 8:1), their situation (poverty, 8:2), their selflessness (beyond their ability, 8:3, 4), and their sacrifice (gave of self, 8:5).

Notice that it was the Macedonians' giving that made those churches famous in the Bible. They not only received, but they gave. They gave voluntarily. They gave because they desired to give. And they gave because they dedicated themselves first.

The grace that God gave to the Macedonians was not so much in material things, for they were extremely poor. Rather, the *grace* Paul spoke of was their salvation and their character of selflessness.

The Macedonians had been going through a "severe trial." This expression is more literally translated, "a great ordeal of affliction." The word *affliction* is from θλίψις, the Greek word we've already seen several times in this epistle that means "crushing grain or grapes." It was a trial of devastation. It was the kind of trial that could have totally crushed the spirit and life out of some people, but not the Macedonians. Their attitude was greater than their situation. Note the contrasts mentioned here that spotlight the bigness of the Macedonian hearts.

Their Situation	Their Attitude
Severe trial	Overflowing joy
Extreme poverty	Rich generosity
As much as they were able	Beyond their ability

The word for *trial* or *ordeal* is the word that was used for evaluating and purifying precious metals. Precious metals are put into fire, which burns off the unworthy stuff that shouldn't be attached to gold and other metals. Sometimes, the primary test that evaluates the worth and genuineness of Christians is the test of the use of their money.

The Greek word for *extreme poverty* is a word that means the deepest and most serious kind of poverty. The picture was one of having hit rock bottom. They were at the bottom of the well, and there was no rope reaching to them. They were so deep in poverty that it did not look as if anyone could get them out of it. In fact, they were in such deep poverty that they were in a position of being beggars asking others to give them aid. What a good excuse to reply, "We are not going to give to the poverty in Judea because we have poverty equal to theirs. You need to be taking up an offering to help us, Paul, instead of having the audacity to ask us to give to someone else." Yet, with their deep poverty, they had an overflowing of joy. That teaches us that Christian joy does not depend upon external activities, but rather internal attitudes. Christian joy does not depend upon being suspended from difficulty, but rather depends upon a superiority over those difficulties. Remember the word for *trial* is a word that means a test for the purpose of approval. What churches do in helping others while they themselves are experiencing hardships may be one of God's best ways to approve or disapprove that congregation. And it may be one of God's best ways to mature that congregation into God's characteristics. It is easy to be selfish when things are tight. We like to take care of number one first; but we should not criticize the church for selfishness, for the church is people—you and me! Do we want to take care of number one first?

Probably part of the Macedonians' joy came from their outreach in giving away with generosity. It is true that there is more joy in giving than in receiving. So the Macedonians, while in the pits themselves, "welled up in rich generosity." The word *generosity* comes from a Greek word that means "with liberality." But that Greek word also means "singleness." The idea is that the Macedonians had set their minds on one thing—helping someone else—being people helpers.

The Macedonians demonstrated three important principles of giving. They gave with the right attitudes, the right actions, and the right priority.

Right Attitudes. They gave joyfully and with generosity, that is, liberality (2 Corinthians 8:2). They gave voluntarily (2 Corinthians 8:3). They considered it a privilege, rather than a burden, to give. They considered it a "service to the saints" (2 Corinthians 8:4).

Right Actions. They gave as much as they were able. In fact, they gave beyond their ability (2 Corinthians 8:3). They begged to be given an opportunity to give (2 Corinthians 8:4).

Right Priority. "They gave themselves first to the Lord" (2 Corinthians 8:5).

It is quite clear that the Macedonians were not owned by their material possessions, but rather owned them. Thus, they were free to use them and dispose of them as they willed. It is one thing to own something. It is quite different, however, for something to own us. Some people may think that they own their businesses, but their businesses really own them. Some people may think that they own their bank accounts, but their bank accounts really own them.

There are three attitudes that we can have about possessions:
1. What is mine is mine and I will keep it.
2. What is yours is mine and I will take it.
3. What is mine is the Lord's and I will share it with others whenever there is a need.

We really see something significant about the heart of the Macedonians when they "urgently pleaded with us for the privilege of sharing in this service to the saints." Probably the apostle Paul felt so badly about their deep poverty that he wanted to take up a collection for them—or at least had decided not to receive a collection from them. But they would have none of it. They begged Paul to allow them to be a part of this great ministry to others. Have we ever seen anyone beg to give in the offering? The fact that the Macedonians did tells us some important characteristics of effective Christianity.

First, Christianity is a *participating relationship*. Second, Christianity is a *ministering relationship*. Both of these are possible because Christianity is a *receiving relationship* (2 Corinthians 8:1). But another aspect of Christianity that cannot be missed is that Christianity is a *personal relationship* (2 Corinthians 8:5). Christians do not just give things in an impersonal way. The Macedonians "gave themselves first to the Lord and then to us." That means that before they gave their money, they gave themselves. But there is something else very important about that notation. Anytime a person gives himself to the Lord, he at the same time offers himself to the Lord's people. It was one act, not two, when the Macedonians gave themselves to "the Lord and then to us." To be open to the Lord is to be open to the Lord's people. To be willing to give oneself to the Lord is to be willing to give oneself to the Lord's people. I cannot say, "I am willing to give myself to the Lord, but not to you." Christianity reaches up and reaches out. Then there can be joy in the midst of a severe trial, and generosity in the midst of poverty. With that in mind, sharing our material needs for others is, indeed, a privilege.

The Motivation of the Church's Past History (8:6, 7)

The effect of the Macedonians' attitude and activity in giving impressed Paul so much that he was more motivated to encourage the Corinthians to complete their collection. In fact, after speaking about the Macedonian situation, he started the next section with the word *so*. That literally introduced a *result* of what Paul had just written. As a result of the effect of the Macedonian's example, Paul urged Titus to bring the Corinthians' act of grace to a completion.

Evidently Titus had talked with the Corinthians about that while he was with them. Then he was going to return to Corinth in order to help orchestrate their completion of the collection before Paul would later arrive.

Paul helped to motivate the Corinthians by reminding them that they had already started this collection and needed to complete it. After hearing about the Macedonians, no Corinthian could claim that he was not in a financial state to do any sharing.

Paul further motivated them by reminding them of how wonderfully they had been progressing in five other areas of their Christian walk:

1. In faith. They had trusted God and trusted Paul so much that they were making life-style changes in accordance with God's will. They evidently had expressed the kind of faith that also allowed many miracles to be done by the members in that congregation (1 Corinthians 13:1-3). The ability to do miracles was a grace-gift from God (1 Corinthians 12:9).

2. In speech. The Corinthians were gifted with prophets. People also spoke in languages they had not learned and with the translation of those languages (1 Corinthians 12:10).

3. In knowledge. The Corinthians had an understanding of the gospel facts and of doctrinal and practical areas (1 Corinthians 12:8; 13:2). Paul acknowledged early in 1 Corinthians that the Corinthians had been enriched in their speaking and knowledge, and that they did not lack any spiritual gift (1 Corinthians 1:5-7).

4. In complete earnestness. The Corinthians had zeal or haste to do what God wanted them to do with a newer life-style (2 Corinthians 7:11).

5. In love. Love had been deficient earlier in the Corinthians' attitudes and activities. That's why Paul wrote to them that great love chapter of 1 Corinthians 13. But that was changing. They were growing in their love for the work of the Lord and in their love for the messengers of God such as Paul.

The Corinthians had not been satisfied in just being possessors of the above five attributes. They were maturing in them. They were growing in them. They were excelling in them. What a magnificent change was taking place. But then Paul asked them to excel also in their grace of giving. To do that would be a further expansion of their faith, speech, knowledge, earnestness, and love. To excel in the grace of giving would also be an evidence of a magnificent change from their former life-style. In 1 Corinthians 6, we see that the Corinthians were not interested in giving, but only in getting. In fact, they would sue each other in order to get their rights. They were willing to "cheat and do wrong" in order to increase their bank accounts and their accumulations. Giving would prove that they had changed in this respect.

So Paul was motivating them by their own recent history. They had been progressing in many areas that they had started. They had also started a collection for the saints a year earlier. So Paul was motivating them to be consistent in their present positive trends. In a sense, he was saying, "You are on a roll. Now keep it up."

The Motivation of the Example of Jesus (8:8, 9)

Paul was not issuing an apostolic command, for he wanted the giving to come from the Corinthians' own free will because they had adopted a life-style closer to God's. This would indeed test the sincerity of their love. The word *test* is the same word mentioned above *(trial)* that was used for the test to prove the legitimacy of precious metals. Consequently, our openness and involvement in sharing to relieve the basic needs of others is an assessment of our legitimate love. The Old Testament is filled with God's caring for hurting people. One cannot read through the book of Acts without seeing that part of the life-style of the early church was to be certain that the poor were cared for. Acts 4:33, 34 is a powerful testimony to this, although it is weakened in most translations including the NIV. Verse 33 reads, "With great power the apostles continued to testify to the resurrection of the Lord Jesus, and much grace was upon them all." Verse 34, in the Greek, begins with the word *for,* which introduces the reason for what had just been said. It had just been written that the apostles continued to testify with great power to the resurrection of Jesus *for* "there were no needy persons among them, for from time to time those who owned lands or houses sold them, brought the money from the sales and put it at the apostles' feet, and it was distributed to anyone as he had need" (Acts 4:34, 35). It was that action with benevolence that gave the early church a powerful testimony to their resurrection life. And it wasn't just a few who did it; "All the believers were one in heart and mind. No one claimed that any of his possessions was his own, but they shared everything they had" (Acts 4:32).

So when Paul was asking the Corinthians to get with it in their benevolence, he was not asking them to go a step beyond the life-style of the early church, but rather get back to what the early church initially demonstrated. And so that should be with us. Many people today rejoice in restoring New Testament Christianity. But it is not restored just because we know facts and have a certain stance on the Bible. New Testament Christianity is not restored until we adopt the life-style, the generosity, the big heart, and the commitment of the early church.

If the love of Christians is sincere, it will be Christ's kind of love. So Paul immediately moved from saying that he was going to test the sincerity of their love to bringing to them the example of Jesus himself. Jesus was a master at caring for the poor at His own expense. The "grace of our Lord Jesus Christ" refers to His generosity in giving. "He became poor, so that you through his poverty might become rich." Jesus became poor in many ways:

1. He became poor as He left Heaven and took on humanity. That was an emptying of himself (Philippians 2:5-11).

2. He became poor in His humiliation.

3. He became poor by not accumulating things for himself, but rather meeting the needs of others.

4. He became poor by voluntarily giving of himself in a ministry of reconciliation.

5. He became poor by voluntarily giving of himself to meet the basic need of others.

6. He became poor by breaking religious traditions of His day and meeting the needs of others in ways not ritually acceptable and on days not ritually acceptable.

Jesus did not do any of that for himself. He did it voluntarily out of the depth of His love. Jesus first of all gave of himself; then He met the needs of others, and that's precisely what the Macedonians had done. And that's the way all of our giving should be done—by the giving of ourselves and then the giving of our possessions that will minister to the benefit of others.

There are several other aspects in which Jesus became poor. These can be seen clearly on the following chart. Jesus' wealth is seen in what He was or had in Heaven with the Father. His poverty is seen in His condition while He was on earth.

Jesus' Wealth	Jesus' Poverty
Source of power	Weak in the eyes of men
Commander	Obedient
King of kings	Servant
God	Man (and God)
Sinless	Sin for us
Health	Bore our infirmity
Honored	Despised
Life	Crucified
Unity with God	Separated from God on the cross
An eternal home in Heaven	No place to lay His head
Glory	A curse—crucifixion
Abundant joy	Carried our sorrow
Loved by God	Smitten by God

Jesus is the greatest model of the person who appears to have nothing but possesses all things. Notice that Jesus' poverty did not last forever. He became poor to make others rich, and in that process, He himself became eternally rich. And so it will be with us. We may not become rich in this lifetime, but who needs to? Life on planet earth is a mere vapor, a second, a breath compared to eternity. If we have been faithful with our little (or much) here on earth, God will grant us overflowing abundance in Heaven, and that will last forever; it will never wear out; it will never be depleted; it will never be stolen; it will never lose its value.

God expects us to use our possessions for the benefit of others. If we do not, then we are selfish. Then our love is not sincere. Then we permit the love of money to lead us into all kinds of evil. Then we become fools like the man in Luke 16, who kept storing up what he had instead of sharing it. Then we become like the rich person in James 5, whose gold and silver rusted and grain rotted while people around him were starving to death.

Elsewhere, Paul summed up this necessity of Christians when he said,

Command those who are rich in this present world not to be arrogant nor to put their hope in their wealth, which is so uncertain, but to put their hope in God, who richly provides us with everything for our enjoyment. Command them to do good, to be rich in good deeds, and to be generous and willing to share. In this way they will lay up treasure for themselves as a firm foundation for the coming age, so that they may take hold of the life that is truly life (1 Timothy 6:17-19).

The reason Christ has made us rich is not so that we will just get richer, fatter, lazier, and less dependent upon God, but that we will have something to share with others. If putting on Christ causes us to have a new heart (and it does), then that heart is a heart of generosity. It would be a shame to have generosity in our hearts and have absolutely nothing with which to express that generosity. So God provides every Christian with something to share with others. Even those who are in "extreme poverty" have something they can share. That is the example of the Macedonians.

It would be advisable for every Christian to set aside a special checking or savings account labeled "For Benevolence Only" and then to use that only for people who have basic needs unmet. And in our world today, because of the economics of the age, because of family split-ups and people's being abandoned, and because of many other tragedies, there are many people who have basic needs unmet all around us. There are people who were born in poverty and have never got out of that. There are diseased people with no income for receiving ease. There are divorced who have literally been financially abandoned by their mates. There are single parents about whom few care anything. There are many people of other races for whom few hands reach out to touch. There are the senior citizens, whose number is multiplying, and many of them are getting deeper in poverty. If the church had done in our lifetime what God speaks so much about in the Old Testament, what Jesus modeled in the Gospels, and what the church did in the Book of Acts, the government would have very little it would have to do in the area of benevolence. But by and large, the church has become disobedient and rebellious from the example of Jesus and from the commands of our Heavenly Father in the area of generosity and benevolence.

Then we wonder why it is difficult to evangelize people in our communities. Some people have been able to write this off by saying such ministry is "social gospel." That is just an excuse to remain stingy. Reaching out to meet the needs of others is really a people ministry. And God specializes in people ministries. It is true that man does not live by bread alone, but it is also true that man does not live long without it.

Although Jesus refused to turn stone into bread in the wilderness, He later refused to turn His back upon people who needed bread (the feeding of the 5000 and later of the 4000). While Jesus refused to turn stone into bread, some restaurants today do the reverse. They turn bread into stone, and that consequently gets thrown away.

The Motivation to Complete Goals (8:10-12)

Setting goals is important for human beings. We work best when we have something out in front of us to accomplish. And it is also important to track how we are doing with those goals and then compare ourselves to that. That is what Paul did here.

The Corinthians had been the first ones to desire to give and then to give. They had led the parade. They had been out front. That may have been the motivation that caused other congregations to get on board, even the Macedonians. Paul probably, as he traveled, shared about how eager the Corinthians had been.

However, something had changed. They had evidently lost both the desiring and the doing. That would have been due to their in-house difficulties that we have already discussed. But now their desire had been resurrected by their repentance. But that desire had not been followed up with the doing (2 Corinthians 8:11). So Paul was simply asking them to finish what they had started. Paul was not suggesting that they give the same amount that others gave. In fact, Paul gave advice that shatters much that is taught in faith promise rallies, "For if the willingness is there, the gift is acceptable according to what one has, not according to what he does not have" (2 Corinthians 8:12).

Paul was not overly impressed that people would promise to give something later with the faith that it might come in. He was impressed that people would give what they presently had. In fact, that can take more faith, for if we give away what we have, then we have to have faith that God will continue to supply us. Farmers express that kind of faith when they put their last seed in the ground. They do that with the faith that the seed will produce many more seeds.

Of course, it is not inappropriate to make a promise to give an amount in the future if God will provide the means. But it is inappropriate to do that if in so doing we refuse to give what we presently have available. If God is able to provide a surplus in the future, then God can also provide what is needed to fill up our lack caused by generosity.

Paul also suggested in this verse that it is not the amount that really matters, but the attitude. In fact, the attitude measures the amount. Jesus taught this in Luke 21:1-4, when He saw a widow put all she had in the temple offering. It was probably the least amount that was put in that day. Many rich people put in large sums, and she put in only a penny's worth. But Jesus remarked, "This poor widow has put in *more* than all the others."

A proper attitude can inspire others to give a larger amount. We have reversed that. We have brought people in front of the audience to give testimonies about the large amounts they are going to give, hoping that their large amounts will inspire others. We are very slow to invite someone up front to give a testimony of a small amount that he plans to give. We need to invite people who have a big attitude about their generosity. It is quite possible that someone with very little—such as a widow or a single parent raising several kids, who could give a testimony about her willingness to give out of her extreme poverty—could inspire more people to be generous than the person who promises $30,000 or $50,000 to a special project.

In death, we will all give up what we won't give up in life. So why not experience some of the joy in living by giving some of that up now? Our attitude with our possessions gives evidence of whether or not God is really in control. God is not in control if money builds our ego, if money corrupts us, if money worries us, if money makes us greedy, or if we think we are the owner of everything that we have.

It is not money that is the root of all evil, but rather the *love of money*. Money does not automatically corrupt. God made Abraham rich. Solomon was the richest man on planet earth. No one is richer than God. God expects Christians to multiply money and use it for good, not just maintain it and hoard it.

The Motivation of Having an Equality in Needs (8:13-15)

Paul was not asking the people to be involved in some kind of religious con-game. Some individuals in organizations thrive off taking money from the poor. While the poor do without, these have lined their pockets and do with plenty.

Although Christianity is to be a life of sharing, that sharing is to be a two-way street. God wants His family to be the kind of family that practices reciprocal giving when the needs change. God does not expect us to have equal goods, but equal care. Our Father does not teach that all of us should have the same provisions, but rather that no one should have basic needs left unmet.

God has provided the means to meet the vital needs of mankind, but He leaves it up to us humans to work with, multiply, cultivate, and distribute what He has provided. What a responsibility God has given to Christians when He inspired Paul to say "At the present time your plenty will supply what they need" (2 Corinthians 8:14). We have people throughout the world in severe need of the most basic item—food—while we in the United States continue to store up grain to keep the price up and then dump it when the grain gets too old. Surely another system could emerge from this Christian nation!

We have enough land along the medians of our freeway system to feed some whole countries if that land were cultivated into wheat, corn, or some other food grain. Why not use some unemployed people, some prisoners, or some people on welfare to plant, cultivate, and harvest the medians along our freeways for the purpose of providing for the needs around the world?

God has indeed given us the land, the resources, and the creativity, if man will only tap it with the sensitivity of his fellowman on his heart.

Paul's quotation of Exodus 16:18 strengthens the idea that we are to have equality in having no lack or need, rather than equality in the amount of goods we possess. For people gathered different amounts of manna in the wilderness. Each person had the amount that he needed for his family. Some took more and some took less, but they were all equal because they all had no lack. God took care of all their needs.

There is another lesson to be gleaned from the Exodus 16 passage: "Don't take advantage of your abundance, and don't feel slighted in your lack." In Exodus 16, God opposed both those who were covetous and those who were complainers. Those who collected more and thought that they would become the rich with manna found that their manna spoiled. And that is the tragic picture of the person in James 5 and of the rich man who refused to share with the beggar Lazarus.

Some have taken this paragraph out of context to say such things as, "No one should have two cars as long as someone has none," or, "No one should have two television sets in his home while there are some who have none." But Paul was not talking about that at all. He was talking about the basic needs of mankind in this passage—hunger. If God's people had always disposed of everything they had in any surplus, then they would not be in as good a position to help when there was a basic need that arose.

In one of the parables, Jesus commended two of His stewards who invested the money they had in a way to double their investments. But Jesus criticized the man who did not invest it, and thus did not increase it. Some of the most generous and helpful people I know are rich people who know how to manage their surplus. They do not get rid of their surplus out of guilt that they have it, but they manage their surplus well and use it not only for themselves but also for the benefit of others. That follows the model of the richest person in the world—God!

God has surplus. God is rich. But God does not use it just for himself. He has a heart sensitive to others in need. And that is the new heart that He puts within Christians. Remember, in Christ we are a new creation.

The Motivation of Planning a Work and Working the Plan (8:16-24)

Planning, organization, and open communication are helpful in the church's program of benevolence. That is what we see in this next section. Paul had established a plan with the Corinthians in 1 Corinthians 16. Now Paul outlined an organized way to complete that plan. Paul sent Titus and other people to Corinth to help with the communication, motivation, and collection of their benevolence.

Just knowing that some other people were coming could be a motivation to the Corinthians. But Paul also let them know that the plan was a plan that guaranteed integrity in the use of funds. They already knew the integrity of Titus, for Titus had just recently been with them. And the mutuality between the Corinthians and Titus must have been great. Paul also mentioned that he was going to send with Titus two "brothers" (2 Corinthians 8:17, 18, 22).

Who was "the brother" (2 Corinthians 8:18)? Many people have been suggested, such as Barnabas, Silas, Erastus, Mark, Trophimus, Aristarchus, Secundus, Sopater of Berea, and Luke. The truth is that we do not know the name of the person, and so anyone's guess is as good as another's. What we know is that this person was evidently well known to the church at Corinth because he was referred to as just "the brother." (It is also possible that he could have been an actual brother to Titus or Paul).

This person was not only known to the church at Corinth but also was praised by all the churches for his service in the gospel. Therefore, this person may have been someone who traveled regularly with Paul, such as Luke.

He was a man of unquestionable integrity. He was not only praised by the churches, but also chosen by the churches to accompany Paul in the collection of monies around the world. The word *chosen* (2 Corinthians 8:19) is a word that literally means "stretching out the hand." So churches probably had actually voted by the raising of hands for this person.

The second "brother" was also unnamed. It is possible that he could have been an actual brother to Paul. But he was probably someone that had traveled with Paul, for he had proved in many ways his zeal for the Lord's work (2 Corinthians 8:22). He was someone who knew the Corinthians well; so he may have been with Paul when Paul was in Corinth for eighteen months, for he had "great confidence" in the Corinthians. Perhaps that was Timothy or Silas.

Both of these two unnamed people are called "representatives of the churches" (2 Corinthians 8:23). The word *representatives* is the Greek word *apostles*. These were called apostles not because they were apostles of Jesus, but rather because they were apostles of churches that chose them. The word *apostle* literally means someone who is sent out by another, one who is on a special mission for another.

There are several characteristics that show that Titus and these two brothers made fantastic team people:

1. They had concern for people (2 Corinthians 8:16).

2. They were praised by the churches.

3. They had a track record of being involved in service to the gospel.

4. They were chosen by the churches. They were not self-imposed leaders.

5. They did what they did for the purpose of honoring the Lord (2 Corinthians 8:19).

6. They had an eagerness to help (2 Corinthians 8:19).

7. They had the kind of integrity that would avoid criticism (2 Corinthians 8:20).

8. They were concerned with pleasing both the Lord and their brothers and sisters (2 Corinthians 8:23).

9. They were zealous or enthusiastic (2 Corinthians 8:22).

10. They had confidence in the church (2 Corinthians 8:22).

11. They recognized whom they represented (2 Corinthians 8:23).

These would not be bad characteristics to look for in staff members of a church today, would they?

There are three significant truths buried within this section. All three have to do with the reason for taking the collection for hungering people in Judea. Here they are:

1. It was a "service to the gospel" (2 Corinthians 8:18). One way we serve the good news is to help people in their basic needs here and now.

2. Administering this collection for the poor was a way "to honor the Lord himself" (2 Corinthians 8:19). It is a dishonor to the Lord when we neglect with our insensitivities the basic needs of people. We honor the Lord when we reach out and meet people's needs, for in doing that, we communicate to others more of the nature of the Lord.

3. The collection for the saints came out of an eagerness to help. That kind of eagerness can grow when we understand that doing it is a way to honor the Lord and is a way to serve the good news that God loves all mankind.

The church can learn from Paul's example of having other people travel with him during the collection. Why was that type of plan chosen? There would be at least four major reasons:

1. For protection, for it would have been unwise to have traveled in that day with a large sum of money without several people accompanying the holder of the money.

2. To detour any potential charges that people might hurl at Paul by suggesting that he would keep the money himself or mismanage it (2 Corinthians 8:20).

3. As a witness to each individual church's response and thus a motivation to the churches by having other people present (2 Corinthians 9:3).

4. To help the individual churches finish the arrangements for the collection (2 Corinthians 9:5).

The church can learn from this plan to put into effect a plan that can keep criticism away from people who handle money received from the church. Such a plan would not be made because the individuals are not trusted, but rather to protect them from undue and unjust criticism from people who may not really know them well. What could such plans include in a local church today?

1. No one person should count the offering by himself. There should always be more than one present when money is counted.

2. No one person should sign checks for the church. Rather, at least two signatures should be required.

3. No one person should carry the offering to the safe until a count is made. At least two people should accompany the offering to a storage place.

Notice that Paul had not only motivated the Corinthians to give by many different ways, but also announced in skeleton form his plan that would help enable them to put the collection together—that involved the coming of certain people, their integrity, and Paul's confidence in the Corinthians.

Summary

1. Grace is not just what we receive, but also what we give.

2. God provides *for* us in order that He can provide *through* us.

3. Our reaction to life does not depend upon the circumstances around us, but the attitudes inside us.

4. God expects every Christian to be involved in helping other people meet their basic needs.

5. Sharing with others involves both proper attitudes and proper activities.

6. The attitudes God loves to see include joy, generosity, considering giving a privilege, and insisting on being included in sharing.

7. God expects Christians to give of themselves before they give of their possessions.

8. God wants us to complete the projects that we start for the benefit of others.

9. Christian maturity involves excelling in the grace of giving as well as other kinds of attitudes and activities.

10. God does not expect equality in the amount, but rather equality in the attitudes of giving.

11. It is not equal sharing (that is, the amount that we give), but rather equal sacrifice.

12. God does not expect people to line their pockets from the generosity of other Christian givers.

13. God never taught that everybody should have the same amount of material possessions. But God does want people to have no lack of basic needs.

14. It is important to have a plan and to work that plan.

15. It is important to motivate people to give, not out of guilt, but out of confidence, out of their love, out of their willingness, out of their desire to honor the Lord, out of their eagerness to help others, out of their desire to excel in every Christian grace, and out of their desire to be an example to others.

16. Sharing with others in need is a way to serve the gospel and a way to honor the character of the Lord.

CHAPTER NINE

Characteristics of People-helper Giving

1 Corinthians 9

There is really no break between the ending of 2 Corinthians 8 and the beginning of chapter 9. The New International translation does not show the connection as clearly as the Greek text does. In the Greek text, chapter 9 begins with the word *for (gar)*. Rather than writing commands for the Corinthians to follow, Paul was sending some personnel to the Corinthian church, *for* he had no need to write them a commanding letter about the service to the saints, because they are already eager to participate.

In these two chapters, we clearly see how one congregation's activities motivate another congregation. The Corinthian church's plans a year ago had evidently motivated the Macedonian church to give. Then the Macedonian churches' practices were motivating the Corinthian congregation. So Paul executed a plan so their previous promises could turn into present reality. That is the real gist of the first five verses of 2 Corinthians 9. But why did Paul execute this plan?

I believe he had three reasons for this plan. First, it was so the Corinthians would not lose the awareness of their responsibility (2 Corinthians 9:1). Second, he wanted to be sure they would not eliminate their influence on others (2 Corinthians 9:2-4). Finally, this plan ensured that their gift would not be a last-minute catch-up, but rather a fulfillment of what they really wanted to do in their hearts (2 Corinthians 9:5).

There are several aspects that a people helper should consider as he contemplates giving. Many of them are listed here in 2 Corinthians 9:

1. An eagerness to help others (9:2).
2. The kind of giving that can cause others to be encouraged (9:2).
3. A readiness to give (9:2).

145

4. An enthusiasm that moves to action (9:2).
5. A giving that allows others to observe (9:4).
6. A fulfilling of promises (9:5).
7. A generous gift (9:5).
8. A gift not given grudgingly (9:5).
9. A gift that is made out of definite decisions (9:7).
10. A gift not given reluctantly (9:7).
11. A gift not given out of compulsion or pressure of the moment (9:7).
12. A cheerful giver (9:7).
13. A gift that trusts in the provisions of God (9:6, 8-11).
14. A gift that is interpreted as a "service" (9:12).
15. A gift that supplies the needs of God's people (9:12).
16. A gift that can cause people to praise God (9:13).
17. A gift that shows we are backing up our confession with obedience (9:13).
18. The attitude that is willing to share with anyone who has need (9:13).
19. A gift that causes other people to recognize the grace of God in the lives of the givers (9:14).
20. A gift that is founded upon being grateful for God's gift to us (9:15).

Proper Preparation (9:1-5)

In the Greek, verses 1 and 3 are very closely tied together. The Greek construction reads this way: "On the one hand, there is no need for me to write to you.... But on the other hand, I am sending the brothers...." Although Paul recognized that there was a readiness on the part of the Corinthians, he also knew that it was important to have people around who could help put that readiness into proper preparation and fulfillment.

Our emotional readiness can die fast if it is not watered. After all, there was a readiness the year before, but that had apparently died out.

The Corinthians did not need a letter concerning the need and ministry, for they knew about that quite well. In fact, they had had information for over a year concerning that. But they did need continual prodding because of the previous interruption. But at that time, the Corinthians were eager to help. Paul wanted that eagerness to be turned into activity. After all, it was the enthusiasm of the Corinthians that stirred other Christians. Now those other Christians needed to see that the Corinthians' enthusiasm had been translated into action.

When a congregation gives to help someone in need, it should do so with the kind of attitude that can cause others to take note and be inspired by it. The giving is not done for the purpose of drawing attention to self, but for the purpose of motivating others. There are some who are so reluctant to let anyone else know what they are doing that they continually quote Jesus' words not to let the right hand know what the left hand is doing. But Jesus spoke that to a people who were probably pointing out what they were doing in order to get rewards for themselves. Paul was talking about a whole different motivation for sharing what one congregation was doing.

There are several congregations today that really inspire other congregations because of their unselfishness. They do not necessarily brag about the amount of money that they are spending on various people, needs, or services, but they are open enough to share that they are actively involved in meeting those needs and providing those services.

Many times, all it takes for one congregation to move out of mere interest to active involvement is to have some people visit that congregation with a bit of prodding. That happens today and it happened then. Paul sent brothers to the Corinthian church to help them get ready and fulfill their previous promises. What the Corinthian church needed was some organization and motivational leadership. Paul wanted to save them from an embarrassing situation, embarrassing for him and also for them. The Corinthian congregation was prepared emotionally—eager, ready, and enthusiastic; they had made promises. Now they needed to be further prepared by proper leadership. That same approach could be used by many congregations today. Sometimes a congregation can be motivated more to give to a stewardship campaign, a special worldwide need, or some other worthy project by having personnel outside the congregation come with some motivational, inspirational, and organizational skills.

The words *generous gift,* found in the NIV, are really the Greek word for blessing. Paul was not asking them to give a neutral gift. The gift they would provide would not be neutral at all. It would indeed be a blessing. It would be a blessing to the givers (2 Corinthians 9:6, 11, 14), it would be a blessing to others (2 Corinthians 9:12), and it would be a blessing to God (2 Corinthians 9:12, 13,

15). That's the reason it should not be "grudgingly given." No blessing should be grudgingly given.

And that is also why the finishing up of their promise should have some preparation to it. It should not be done in a hasty last-minute effort. It should not be given in response to the heat of some emotional, psychological appeal. If that happens, then the amount could be begrudged by the giver later. The giving should not be forced. There will be no emotional picking of pockets for this collection. And there should never be any emotional picking of pockets in the church. The emphasis here is upon a calculated, systematic giving out of people's desire. Although Paul did want the giving to be generous, he wanted it to be conscientiously thought out and deliberate. He wanted them to give what they had promised. That's all. They had promised the kind of gift that would be a blessing to others; so he wanted them to perform that kind of giving.

Proper Attitudes (9:6, 7)

Paul's first point is that Christians should have the attitude that our giving does not deplete our resources. Proverbs says, "A generous man will himself be blessed, for he shares his food with the poor" (Proverbs 22:9).

Paul pointed out that one does not withhold sowing in order to keep a good supply of grain for himself. To do so would be poor stewardship—in agape as well as in agriculture. The farmer who does not use his seed will lose it. There is a relationship between sowing and reaping. Liberal sowing makes it possible for liberal harvesting. And liberal giving will not hurt the self. Oh, to believe that!

First-century farmers took part of their harvest each year and set it aside for seed for the next season. The rest they used for food. Wouldn't it have been foolish for a farmer to set aside only a meager supply for seed so that he could have more food to supply his immediate needs. He might have eaten well for a while, but then he could only "sow sparingly" the next year and would not have enough come harvest. Or wouldn't it have been foolish for a farmer to refuse to plant all the seed he had set aside for sowing because to do so would mean that he now had no seed in the storage bin? A farmer with faith in God would put his last seed in the ground, knowing that only as he did would that seed be blessed and would the fruit of it be a blessing to many others. And the Christian with faith in God knows that immediate gratification and having a reserve supply are not as important as providing for the needs of God's kingdom.

However, the blessings of reaping come not just by right actions—sowing seed—but also by right attitudes. In 2 Corinthians 9:7, Paul suggested the following right attitudes: decisiveness, willingness, non-compulsion, and cheerfulness.

First, let's look at *decisiveness.* A Christian's giving should be a considered giving: "Each man should give what he has decided in his heart to give." The giving should not be out of the impulsiveness of the moment. To "decide," in the Greek, is to "choose beforehand." This is not the last-minute emotional decision that comes close to having a salesman come to the door and emotionally sell a product that the buyer discovers soon afterwards that he really did not want. To decide "in the heart" means to think about it, to plan about it, to research the need, to pray about it, and otherwise give careful consideration to the matter. God wants us to be wise stewards, not just hasty ones.

The next attitude is that of *willingness:* ". . . not reluctantly," Paul said. The Greek word for *not reluctantly* literally means not out of grief or sorrow. Some people give out of an appeal and then immediately hurt emotionally because they gave. Some people hurt anytime they give. That does not mean that they hurt financially, but they hurt emotionally. The Macedonians were as poor as people could be, but they were not hurt financially because they gave. In fact, they would have been hurt (emotionally) if Paul had not accepted their gift (2 Corinthians 8:2-5).

While some people hurt emotionally anytime they give, other people give *until* they hurt. That is, they give until they begin to hurt financially. These are the generous givers. They do not hurt emotionally, for they are cheerful givers. But they give beyond their ability (2 Corinthians 8:13). But still other people hurt *until* they give. That is, they are so sensitive to those needs that they hurt with those people who have needs—they hurt to give. They ache to give. They are eaten up on the inside with the motivation to give. And that hurt motivates their giving. These people have a "compulsion," but it is not a compulsion that has been manufactured by outside emotional appeals. It is the inner compulsion of the love of Christ welling up inside of their souls.

The third attitude is represented by Paul's words, *"not under compulsion."* However, Paul was not referring to the inner compulsion that comes from love, but rather the external compulsion that comes from manipulative pressure. This describes someone who is so pressured to give that he has to give in order to get out from under the pressure. This kind of person is agitated and frustrated into giving.

Finally, Paul urged *cheerfulness* in giving: "For God loves a cheerful giver." The word for *cheerful* comes from the Greek word *hilaron,* from which we get our word *hilarious.* God wants us to be "hilarious" givers. The cheerful giver is the person who sizes up the need, considers his means, gives out of love, gives in order to be of service, and does it all voluntarily. We are all to give out of love, not out of law.

Notice that Paul never once mentioned any kind of percentage in this chapter. Using a percentage (such as ten percent or any other percent) can be damaging to the Christian. For some, it causes guilt if they are not up to that percentage. Others use it as a judgmental device for judging their brothers and sisters. While it is good for each Christian to have his own percentage, it is unwise for the church to dictate a percentage to its members. God loves a "cheerful giver," not necessarily a set percentaged giver.

A thought-out, planned, voluntary, systematic giving will help the cheerfulness.

Proper Trust (9:8-11)

Our giving should not be done with threats, but rather with trust. We give with trust in God. What do we trust about God in our giving? We trust that God provides, God multiplies, and God enriches (2 Corinthians 9:8-11).

If we are open to God, He can provide through us cooperatively the means to meet any need. The result of receiving God's blessings is not for Christians simply to enjoy those blessings for themselves, but also to share those blessings with others. This does not mean that Christians should not enjoy the abundant life. It does not mean Christians should never buy something that would be considered a luxury. Those who think like this do not understand our Heavenly Father, nor the way He delights in our enjoying planet earth. But God does provide for us so that we will have all we need to "abound in every good work." And doing that gives us joy as it gives God joy. We are made in the image of God, and our enjoyment comes only as we live out that image. And God's image involves unselfishness.

Paul quoted Psalm 112:9 here, a Psalm that speaks about a person who trusts in God. God scatters His gifts to the poor, and His righteousness endures forever through His people. He provides to us so that He can distribute through us (2 Corinthians 9:9).

God multiplies our resources so that through us the poor can have their needs met. God might multiply our resources by changing our priorities so that we have more available to give away. For instance, a person might buy a used car instead of a new one so that he can use the balance in unselfish benevolence.

No farmer got his seed without God. Where did the farmer get his seed? He got it from other seeds that were sown. But how did those seeds that were sown grow? God provided the rain and the nourishment. Here is a beautiful example of the principle of giving. The seed is supplied to the farmer as he puts it into the ground. He may wipe out his entire seed-savings account by putting his last seed into the earth, but he is not afraid to do that because he knows the power that awaits it. So should the Christian know the power of God as our resource. For as God does what He does for the farmer's resources, He promises to do that for the Christian who is generous and cheerful. Not only does God "increase your store of seed," but He will also "enlarge the harvest of your righteousness" (2 Corinthians 9:10).

Proverbs states that anytime we give to the poor, we are making a loan to God, and God will pay that back (Proverbs 19:17). Seed grows only when it is planted, not when it is kept in storage bins. But how does the seed of our giving increase with dividends? That happens because God increases the fruits of our righteousness. He does things in the lives of people we help. He does things in our lives when we help. No one can purchase those dividends, for they are God-provided. When God says "You will be made rich in every way" (2 Corinthians 9:11), He does not necessarily mean that we are going to have more money in the bank. But we can be rich in attitudes, in generosity, in cheerfulness, in satisfaction, in meaningfulness, in spiritual growth, in mental health, and in social sensitivity.

Proverbs talks about a person who appears to be poor, but is very rich. Jesus himself was poor materially, but was extremely rich with the above characteristics. The person who has the above characteristics is a generous person and meets more needs than a mere bank account could ever make possible.

Results of Giving (9:12-15)

Living to help meet peoples' needs is a "service" that provides many results:

1. It meets the needs of people.
2. It causes people to give thanksgiving to God, so God is blessed.
3. It causes people to praise God, so God is honored.
4. It causes Christians to back up their confession of the gospel with an obedience of life. That confirms our Christian walk. It is one thing to talk the walk, but another to walk the talk.
5. It causes other people to pray for the giver. That increases fellowship across people lines. It breaks down some barriers. It crushes walls. It helps eliminate prejudices.

The opposite of the above is true, however. Sadly, the person who does not give in the way Paul described in this chapter refuses service. He refuses to meet the needs of God's people. He prevents God from getting thanksgivings. He prevents God from receiving the honor He deserves. He fails to confirm his Christian life-style, and he loses out on having people pray for him. Thus, a selfish man is never rich, regardless of the amount of money he has in banks, stocks, real estate, bonds, or other physical wealth.

Anyone who helps prevent the above positive things from happening is a poor man indeed. If he lives long enough, he will eventually discover that there is little meaning in life for him. There is little purpose that gives him satisfaction and joy. Many multi-millionaires have died in isolation, tremendously depressed.

The last verse of this chapter is a bedrock verse that undergirds everything about giving that has been said in 2 Corinthians 8 and 9. All of our giving should rest upon our gratitude to God for His "indescribable gift." That gift spotlights Jesus Christ. It is an indescribable gift because all the words in the world cannot exalt the greatness of what God has done for us in Christ and what God continues to do for us. Were the oceans filled with ink, it would not be enough to write about this gift of God for us.

God's "indescribable gift" fulfilled every characteristic of giving that we have seen in 2 Corinthians 8 and 9. He gave all that He had. He didn't just give away something, He gave himself first to us. His giving was an act of grace on His part. God not only excelled in all other characteristics, but also excelled in the "grace of giving." He was not commanded to give, but gave voluntarily for our benefit. He planned to give. He promised that gift. He was eager to give that gift. He was enthusiastic to give that gift. His enthusiasm was translated into action. He was ready to give the gift. It was a generous gift. God did not give it grudgingly. He gave generously. He did not give reluctantly. He did not give under compulsion, except the inner compulsion of love. He gave cheerfully. God's giving did not make Him poor. His gift supplies our needs for salvation. His gift is a service. His gift brings thanksgiving to Him. His gift brings honor to Him. His gift is open not only to us, but "to everyone else." His gift causes prayers from us to go to Him.

"Thanks be to God for his indescribable gift!" And one way to thank God is to allow our hearts to be filled with the kind of gratitude that spills over into generosity for the needs of others.

Freely, you have received. Freely, give. This world would experience a new revolution if every Christian began to give as God outlines. This world needs that revolution. We have harbored stinginess, greed, warfare, stealing, bribery, envying, jealousy, neglect, hatred, and hoarding too long. Let's be a part of a new revolution, and let it start today—in your heart and mine!

CHAPTER TEN

The Nature of Paul's Warfare

2 Corinthians 10

Beginning with chapter 10, this letter to the Corinthians takes a different twist. Both the tone and the content have shifted. Chapters 10—13 are a bit more harsh, a bit more blunt, and a bit more direct than the rest of the letter. The subject moves from the Corinthians to Paul himself. Paul seems to have been a bit more impatient in this last section than in the preceding chapters. He wrote in more of a confrontational mode.

Because of this shift, in both emphasis and emotion, many scholars suggest that chapters 10—13 were not originally a part of this letter. Some believe that this last section was really the distressing letter to which Paul referred in 2 Corinthians 2:3, 4, supposing that it was later found and then attached to 2 Corinthians. For this reason, in fact, some commentators begin their commentaries on 2 Corinthians with chapter 10.

Others suggest that the first nine chapters were written to the church while chapters 10—13 were written primarily to Paul's opponents. Therefore, having two different audiences accounts for the two different emphases.

However, there is no ancient manuscript that has chapters 10—13 separated from the rest of 2 Corinthians. Nor are there any ancient manuscripts that place these chapters in a different location from where they are now. There is nothing in this section about disciplining an offender, which would have been a part of the topic of Paul's lost letter (2 Corinthians 2:4-6). Paul referred to sending Titus and the brother in 2 Corinthians 12:18, which shows that this is a continuation of what Paul had previously written.

Then why the change in tone and content? The change was not the result of two different letters or two different audiences, but rather a shift in emphasis to the same audience in the same letter.

The emphasis was changed because there was a need for a change. And why not meet that need in this same letter?

Although the church as a whole had repented and turned to Paul, which gave Paul great encouragement and comfort (2 Corinthians 1:9), there were certain ones in Corinth who had not made that change. There seem to have been some who were challenging Paul's work. They were involved in a counter-mission. Some were questioning Paul's character and integrity (2 Corinthians 10:1). They apparently wanted Paul to be more militant in the show of his authority (2 Corinthians 10:2-6). They looked on the surface of things and were judgmental of others, trying to determine who was not in Christ based upon evaluating others by themselves (2 Corinthians 10:7). They seem to have been the kind of people who loved to tear other people down (2 Corinthians 10:8) and to compare themselves with others (2 Corinthians 10:12). They were trying to lead the Corinthians away from the central teachings of Christ (2 Corinthians 11:1-4), claiming that they themselves were "super-apostles" with greater authority than Paul's (2 Corinthians 11:5, 6). They criticized Paul because he did not receive money for his preaching in Corinth (2 Corinthians 11:7-12). They disguised themselves as apostles when they were not (2 Corinthians 11:13-15). These people were bombarding the Corinthians with boasting about themselves and about their accomplishments. Evidently, their boasting was having some effect; so Paul also began to address that issue in this final section.

Why was the boasting of these false apostles working? They were probably using ecstatic experiences to help their case (2 Corinthians 12:11, 12). They probably repeated their justifications for a deviant life-style long enough that people began to believe them (2 Corinthians 12:21). They evidently used strong rhetoric, and thus criticized Paul because he did not (2 Corinthians 11:6). They undermined Paul and thus built up themselves. They built upon what others had done (2 Corinthians 10:13, 14). Apparently, they talked about how much they had suffered for Christ (2 Corinthians 11:22-29). They evidently demonstrated strength in health and other matters, and so criticized Paul for being "weak" (2 Corinthians 12:7-9).

All of the above rationale can have powerful influence upon a gullible audience. And every one of the above approaches is being used today by certain television, radio, and pulpit preachers.

Paul realized the danger of this kind of activity in the church. It could undermine his work. It could turn the minds of people away from his apostleship. It could turn people's affections and priorities toward false teachers. These false teachers were probably Judiazers (2 Corinthians 11:22), who were extremely uncomfortable with people's becoming Christians and claiming a kinship with God the Father without coming through Judiasm first.

It is quite clear that there were some people in the church who had not repented of "the impurity, sexual sin and debauchery in which they have indulged" (2 Corinthians 12:21). Those were probably the false teachers, for it was not so much a different doctrine but a different life-style (sin) that was keeping them from repenting and accepting Paul's teaching. The number of people who had not changed were in the minority, and Paul gave a great deal of time to countering their claims. That was because a little leaven can soon spread throughout the entire batch of dough. A little corruption could soon spread throughout the entire church. The Corinthians were making progress, and Paul wanted them to continue and not slip back into their former frame of mind. The state of obedience of most of the church should not be weakened by the state of disobedience by a few.

Because the majority had repented, had changed, and were in a frame of mind to do what was right, Paul was ready to discipline verbally those few who continued to be obstinate. He knew that the majority would back him and affirm the content of chapters 10—13. If Paul had written this before most of the church had changed, then most of the church would have rejected what he had to say and become defensive for those involved in a counter-Christian culture. So Paul first worked on an inner renewal of the majority in the church. When that happened, the church had a solid platform to support Paul in disciplining those perverters who were continuing to be a pain.

Actually, chapters 10—13 do not make a total break from what Paul wrote in chapters 1—9, as several scholars suggest. There is much in the first nine chapters that directly anticipates where Paul would go in this section. This was no afterthought of Paul's mind. This was not a "P.S." that he tacked on just to fill up space. He knew he was going to move into this area when he started the letter. There are several passages in the first nine chapters that clearly anticipate what Paul intended to develop further in the last section, as the following chart demonstrates.

How 2 Corinthians 1—9 Anticipates Chapters 10—13	
Earlier Passage	**Anticipated Passage**
1:6	12:7ff; 13:3, 4
1:9, 10	11:22ff (boasting)
1:12	10:2, 3
1:17	10:9, 10
1:13	10:1, 9, 10
1:24	1:12ff, 12:14, 15; 13:10
2:1-4	10:1f, 9
Chapter 3	Chapters 10—13 (the Judaizer situation)
3:1-2	12:11
3:12	10:9, 10
4:2	10:1, 2; 12:17ff
4:5	10:12
4:16	Chapters 10—13 (especially 11:3)
4:15	11:7-9
5:1-10	Paul's boasting in chapter 11
5:16-21	12:19-21
6:3-10	10:1, 2 and the boasting in Chapter 11
6:14—7:1	Chapters 10—13
7:2	Chapters 10—13 (especially 13:2; 11:9; 12:17)
7:8	10:10

So to suggest that chapters 10—13 make a total break of both the tone and emphasis of the first nine chapters is misleading indeed. Paul had carefully dropped enough seeds in the first nine chapters to give the Corinthians some hints about what was coming in 10—13.

Evidently, some people wanted Paul to be far more militant than he was. So in 2 Corinthians 10, Paul defended his kind of warfare. Within this chapter, he was defending the kind of battle he was in, his kind of disposition, his commitment, his style of leadership, and his security.

Paul's Battle (10:1-6)

Christians are indeed in a warfare. The New Testament uses many terms that were warlike terms in the first century. *Lord, army, soldiers, armor, shield, helmet, sword, fight, good fight, guard, be on the alert, wage war,* and *fellow soldiers* were all military terms. But the Christian battle is not like the battles of the world. There are several differences, including the following:

1. The Christian battle is not against people (Ephesians 6:12).
2. The Christian battle is never for self-defense.
3. The Christian battle is never to expand territory for self.
4. The Christian does not battle with the same kind of weapons as the world.
5. The Christian does not take the same kind of captives as the world does.
6. The Christian does not fight with the same disposition as the world.
7. The leaders of the Christian battle do not have the same rough and tough character as the world.
8. The Christian does not seek to be promoted to the ranks that people in the world's armies do.

Evidently, some of the rabble-rousers within the Corinthian church were far more militant than Paul and criticized Paul's mild stance. But Paul did not defend himself against that. In fact, he started this section by making it clear that it was through the "meekness and gentleness of Christ" that he appealed to them. The word *meekness* was a Greek word used to refer to wild horses that had been tamed.

The meek are not weak, but rather people who have their spirits under control. A meek person can keep his cool while others are being provoked. Meekness is the opposite of self-assertion. The meek person ceases to think of himself first. The meek person's pride has been crucified with Christ. The meek person accepts the hard knocks of life and seeks to learn from them without kicking back or without carrying resentment or revenge. A wild horse cannot stand the slightest spur. He will buck and kick and try to destroy. But the tame horse can take the jabs of the spur and will seek to please his master.

The meek person does not measure events according to how they affect his comfort and self-esteem. The meek person looks at life through God's eyes of love and seeks to serve situations and people with that love. The Greeks used the word to describe soothing things such as smooth winds, soothing medicine, tame animals, and calm people. So the meek person is someone who is soothing, smoothing (in a helpful way), tame, and calm.

Gentleness comes from meekness. Gentleness means the ability to put up with unbearable situations. It means consideration for others. A meek and gentle person will feel the wrong and feel it quickly and bitterly. Meek and gentle people are not blind or unreal, but they will not pay back the wrong they feel was done to them. They will not pay back the hurt they feel with hurt. They will not go after the wrongdoer with the purpose of destroying him. Instead, they are full of pity and love for the people who may have even wronged them. While some people charge meekness and gentleness to weakness, Paul charged it to Christ. These are Christlike characteristics (Matthew 11:29). In fact, meekness is a part of the wisdom that comes from above (James 3:17). It is a characteristic of the Holy Spirit (Galatians 5:23). The meek win over the monsters, the mild win over the mad. The calm win over the calamitous.

An army will take on the characteristics of their leaders. Who wants to be a part of an army whose leaders are meek and gentle? Wouldn't that mean that the army would be run over and defeated? Who wants to be a part of a church whose leaders are meek and gentle? Wouldn't that mean the church would surely lose in the midst of alien territory? Both Christ and Paul wanted to be a part of that spiritual army—the army of meekness.

Some had charged Paul with being "timid" when face to face, but "bold" when away (2 Corinthians 10:1). They saw in his letters some pretty strong words, but suggested that when he came face to face with people, he melted away. The Greek word for *timid* is literally the word for being humble. The Greeks did not consider humility to be a virtue, but rather a characteristic to despise and reject. But humility is not a way to lose; rather, it is the way to win. The Bible is clear that God will exalt the humble.

One of the reasons Paul's disposition may have seemed different when he was present with people from what his letters suggested is that Paul's letters changed people. Thus, he did not have to come on as strong when he was with the people. They had already made adjustments in their lives. Paul made it clear that if he did have to do so, he would (2 Corinthians 10:2). He was not playing the cat and mouse game. He was not one way when he was at a safe distance from people and then a different way when he was up close. That's the way a lot of people live their lives, but Paul did not "live by the standards of this world" (2 Corinthians 10:2). And because he did not live by the standards of this world, he was not fighting the kind of battles that were going on in the world.

Paul then described the kind of battle he was in. He affirmed that he was living in the world (2 Corinthians 10:3). No Christian can escape living in this world. Although we live in the flesh, we do not have to be controlled by the flesh. Although we live in the midst of a pagan society, we do not have to be conformed to that society. We can walk around in the flesh without soldiering according to the flesh. That is what Paul was getting at when he said, "We do not wage war as the world does" (2 Corinthians 10:3).

What does it mean in this context to "wage war as the world does"? The rest of this section (2 Corinthians 10—13) gives us some of the specifics. People of the world wage war in this way:

1. They look only on the outward circumstances (10:7).
2. They use authority to tear down people (10:8).
3. They terrify people with words (10:9).
4. They measure themselves by themselves (10:12).
5. They take credit for what other people have done (10:13-15).
6. They live and react out of human jealousy (11:2).
7. They preach another "Jesus" (11:4).
8. They demonstrate a different spirit than the Holy Spirit (11:4).
9. They water down the gospel (11:4).
10. They depend too much upon the oratorical skills (11:6).
11. They have an undue demand for money—self-assertiveness (11:7).
12. They are deceitful—they are fakes (11:13-15).
13. They boast according to outward accomplishments (11:18).
14. They exalt self (11:20).
15. They take advantage of people by manipulation (11:20).
16. They depend upon false and superficial sensationalism (12:12).
17. They seek what belongs to people for themselves—their property, possessions, and the like (12:14).
18. They are crafty (12:16).
19. They use other people to take advantage of people (12:17).
20. They are self-defensive (12:19).
21. They are quarrelsome (12:20).

The reason Christians do not wage war as the world does is that we have a different Commander in Chief (Jesus Christ), a different power (the Holy Spirit), different weapons (2 Corinthians 10:4), a different battleground (the thoughts of people), and a different goal (to take every thought obedient to Christ, 2 Corinthians 10:5). The weapons are outlined in Ephesians 6:14-20. Those weapons include truth, righteousness, the gospel, faith, salvation, the Word of God, and prayer.

The power that gives victory is "divine power" (2 Corinthians 10:4). It is not the power of swords, bombs, or planes, but the power of God's character living inside the Christian. The characteristics of that power are listed in Galatians 5:22, 24: love, joy, peace, patience, kindness, goodness, faithfulness, gentleness, and self-control. Jesus listed other characteristics of the "divine power" in Matthew 5:3-10. Peter made it clear that God's "'divine power' has given us everything we need for life and godliness through our knowledge of him who called us by his own glory and goodness," for we have become participants in the "divine nature" (2 Peter 1:3, 4).

Some of that divine nature and power are described as faith, goodness, knowledge, self-control, perseverance, godliness, brotherly kindness, and love (2 Peter 1:5-7). Those are the winning characteristics in the world.

These are the characteristics that can "demolish strongholds" (2 Corinthians 10:4). The word for *stronghold* is the word that refers to the kinds of fortresses in which the enemy is dug in and feels secure. While there are strongholds made out of mortar and brick, Paul was speaking about the strongholds that are made in men's minds—their pride, prejudices, and evil social customs. The enemy to Christianity comes in thoughts, not tanks; in pride, prejudice and principles, not in planes; in attitudes, not in antiaircraft. These are the obstacles that keep people prisoners of war of Satan, and hinder them from becoming free in the gracious liberty and love of our Heavenly Father.

The Christian takes a stand against "arguments and every pretension that sets itself up against the knowledge of God." The goal of the Christian battle is to "take captive every thought to make it obedient to Christ" (2 Corinthians 10:5). Satan is after the minds of all people. He poisons people's minds. The tragedy of that is that as a person thinks within himself, so he is. When the devil has a person's mind, he has the whole person. When God has the person's mind, He has the whole person. That is why *repentance* literally means a change of mind. A change of mind always involves a change of manners. The mind is the center of the person's whole being. It is affected by and affects emotions, thought patterns, objectivity, subjectivity, and physical well-being.

As the devil affects a person's mind, so does God. The Christian faith produces an outlook on the world based upon facts and experiences that make sense.

The way the Christian demolishes arguments is not by more arguments, not by self-defense, not by a new system of intellectual philosophy, but rather by pointing people to Jesus Christ—His attitude, His activities, His life-style. Then Christians back up the declaration with a demonstration of a newness of life that loves God, loves self, and loves other people. To the inadequate and incomplete philosophy of life that many people have, the Christian brings the knowledge of God in Jesus Christ. And as that happens, the Holy Spirit convicts people by changing their minds about sin, righteousness, and judgment (John 16:8).

When arguments and pretensions set themselves up against the knowledge of God, then planet earth becomes more degenerate, people are taken advantage of, and the world is a worse place in which to live.

While it is easy to think that Paul was talking about bringing every thought of the non-Christian to obedience to Christ, we must remember that he was writing this to the church. There are many within the church who have not yet allowed their thoughts to become obedient to the Commander in Chief, Jesus Christ. Many church fights and factions are based upon arguments and pretensions that are not in accordance with the knowledge of God. And some leaders are not interested in taking the time to study what the Bible says about various issues. They have made up their minds and their minds are going to be in control of the rest of the church. It is time that every leader in the church understand that the leaders' minds and the other people's minds alike are to be obedient to the knowledge of God. When that doesn't happen, there comes a time when discipline must be issued—to leader or non-leader—to anyone who is not allowing his thoughts to line up with God's.

Paul spoke about the time of discipline in 2 Corinthians 10:6. He knew how to be severe with people who were not permitting their minds to be obedient to Christ. But he would not permit that discipline to be premature or to be done in such a way as to include the innocent along with the guilty. He had given the Corinthians time to change their minds. And when everyone who would change had changed, then Paul would bring severe discipline to those who refused to change. When Paul said, "Once your obedience is complete," he was not necessarily meaning that everybody would obey. Rather, he was referring to the obedience of everyone who was willing to obey. He would allow enough time for changes to take place. He would allow enough time for people to pray over the issues. He would allow enough time for people to evaluate the alternatives. Then he would have a proper platform to deal with those who continued to be disobedient to the thoughts of God. That was a part of Paul's meekness and gentleness.

So we see in this paragraph three things about Paul's warfare:
1. His disposition—meekness and gentleness.
2. His strategy—to use the "divine power" of God, which refers to God's nature.
3. His goal—to take every thought obedient to Christ.

Isn't that a different goal than many of us have as leaders in the church? Sometimes our goal is to build buildings, to increase the membership numbers, and to see our projects reach completion the way we have them outlined. But the goal of every program in the church should be designed to bring peoples' minds into conformity with God's. That is done by bringing the knowledge of God to people. And the knowledge of God comes in a person—Jesus Christ. The church is to bring His presence to people.

Perhaps one reason this does not happen as it should is because the church preaches too much about things, plans, programs, and creeds than about the person of Jesus.

Some people hear more about baptism than Jesus. Some people hear more about prophecy and the end times than Jesus. Some people hear more about money than Jesus. Some people hear more about social issues than Jesus. Some people hear more about a particular millennial stance than Jesus. We are not going to win the battle unless our disposition, strategy, and goal are the same as Paul's.

Paul's Leadership (10:7-11)

Paul discussed the kind of "military" leader he was under three headings: his identity, his authority, and his integrity.

Paul's identity is seen in his statement, "We belong to Christ" (2 Corinthians 10:7). Evidently, Paul's opponents were claiming to be in Christ, but disclaiming that Paul was. Those opponents had evidently used some kind of superficial criteria for evaluating who was or was not in Christ. That is why Paul said, "You are looking only on the surface of things." It is so easy for Christians to set up external tests that are quite unreal for determining who is or is not in Christ.

While Paul did not un-church his opponents for taking that stance, he was not going to allow them to un-church him either. No one has a right to set up his own checklist and then write people out of the family of God because they do not square with that particular checklist. Everybody's checklist is related to Scripture, but often the Scripture does not allow those items to be used to identify whether or not a person is or is not a Christian. For instance, some people think a person has to speak in tongues to be a Christian. Others think that a person has to take the Lord's Supper *every* Sunday to be a Christian. Some think a person has to belong to a particular brand of church to be a Christian. Others think a person has to lift up his hands in prayer or praise to be a Christian. Others think that if a person drinks a glass of wine, he cannot be a Christian. Some think a person cannot dance and be a Christian. Years ago, some people taught that you could not go roller skating and be a Christian. Some people think that your style of clothing or style of hair is a checklist item. The list goes on and on and on. Most of those lists look "only on the surface of things." It is time for Christians to live out the old slogan, "In essentials, unity; in nonessentials, liberty; in all things, love." Despite differences in externals, Christians need to be able to affirm, "I belong to Christ as much as another."

Paul then moved to discuss his authority. Some people have authority because they have claimed it for themselves, and some people use their authority for the purpose of taking advantage of people by tearing them down. Some people are inconsistent with their authority—powerful when talking behind someone's back, but a milk toast when meeting him face to face. Paul rebuked all of that. The source of Paul's authority was Jesus Christ (2 Corinthians 10:7). The purpose of Paul's authority was to build people up, not tear them down (2 Corinthians 10:8). And Paul was consistent with his authority whether present or absent from people (2 Corinthians 10:9-11).

While some people tried to undermine Paul's authority by suggesting that he was not in Christ, other people evidently tried to undermine Paul's authority by suggesting that he was not militant enough with it. But Paul affirmed that God had given him authority for the purpose of building people up, not for tearing them down (2 Corinthians 10:8). And he was not going to alter that purpose. Paul did not try to scare people into repentance. He did not try to whip people down and then reach down and pick them up as their "savior," nor did he express his authority with an authoritarian voice and speech. Evidently, Paul was not an A + student in power of persuasive speech. He was good with a pen, but did not evidently match up to other people in that day with his speaking ability. So some people criticized that difference (2 Corinthians 10:10).

Paul made it clear that a person's authority is not measured by how loud, offensive, abusive, obnoxious, or mean a person can get with his speech. Paul was committed to not taking advantage of people by his power of public speaking. But he did want people to know that what he said he meant and what he meant he said. He meant what he said in person and he meant what he said with pen (2 Corinthians 10:11).

There are two truths that we need to glean from this section about Paul's speech. First, each of us needs to be full of integrity—that is, to mean what we say and say what we mean. We must not alter our meaning according to the situation. Second, we need to learn that it is not in the impressiveness or eloquence of our speech that the gospel breaks through, but by the power of the Holy Spirit. The Word must be exalted, not our words. Because we have put so much emphasis upon words, it is tempting to be forceful in the pulpit, but to be weak in personal living. It is tempting to be brave when declaring the truth from a distance, but be cowardly when face to face with individuals on a one-to-one basis. Sometimes our conduct in sermons is a disgrace. At other times, our conduct in the streets is a disgrace. To be possessed by the Spirit is the secret of being a persuasive person for God. God needs speakers who are anointed by Him.

Paul's Security (10:12-18)

Paul did not rest his security upon such superficial criteria as his speaking ability (2 Corinthians 11:6), or in how he stacked up in comparison with other people (2 Corinthians 10:12). Nor did he cave in to a false sense of security, but stayed committed to a sense of real security (2 Corinthians 10:17, 18). Many leaders in their warfare try to promote themselves in order to get promotions. They do it by comparing themselves with others, particularly others who will make them look good (2 Corinthians 10:12), boasting about things beyond their limits (2 Corinthians 10:13), and taking credit for work done by others (2 Corinthians 10:15)—many officers in the military willingly take credit for work that privates, corporals, and NCO's have really produced.

Anyone who compares himself by others is without understanding. God has made each person different and has gifted each person differently. Comparison with others may be flattering, but it is false, and the fact that we do it demonstrates our blindness to reality. It is time for churches to quit doing that with other churches. It is time for preachers to quit doing that with other preachers. It is time for Christian musicians to quit doing that with other musicians.

As we should not compare ourselves with others, neither should we compare one person with another person and then decide which person has more functional value in God's kingdom. Paul addressed that activity in 1 Corinthians 3. It is so easy to stack one preacher against another and make unfair conclusions. God can work effectively through different kinds of personalities. Every person is so different from every other person that each person has a different set of fingerprints. No two people have the same.

When a person is conceived, he receives one half cell from each parent. Programmed in that new cell are all the potential physical characteristics of his past ancestry. If he had a relative three hundred years ago that was 7'1" tall, that person would have one chance of being that tall. Someone has calculated that the number of options a person has to draw from is 240 plus 250 billion zeros. (It would take a person 34,000 years just to write all the zeros mechanically.) No two people can ever be exactly alike.

We are far too quick to see something in one person's personality that we do not like and then to write him off. Some members may not like an outgoing preacher who moves among the congregation and shakes hands with people. But what right do we have to not be open for him to minister to us? God lives inside of that personality, and God's love lives inside of us. So we must allow God's love to flow outside of us to the different people around us. The Holy Spirit is in us partly to give us God's character to maintain the unity of the Spirit amid all of the differences that exist among human beings.

It is also time for each Christian to recognize the gifts that God has given to him and to be satisfied and content working in those gifts without claiming that he can do more than what he is presently doing or should be doing.

It is also time that we quit taking credit for what others have done and learn to honor other people in the church. Many people in congregations are doing wonderful things behind the scenes, but getting little praise from the pulpit or from any other avenue of communication. Some senior pastors take credit for what associates are doing. That cuts into a harmonious team ministry.

Every Christian should want other Christians to succeed in their people-helping activities and praise them when that work is being done. We must realize that the church is made up of various individuals with various gifts and that the church needs the functioning of each one. So we are not to evaluate our superiority or inferiority by what others are accomplishing or not accomplishing.

Although Paul was confident that the Corinthians' faith would grow (2 Corinthians 10:15), he would not take credit for it. Not only Paul, but many others had invested their lives and activities in the Corinthian congregation. However, the growth of the Corinthians' faith did affect Paul in a positive way: "Our area of activity . . . will greatly expand." A positive change of one person will help to expand the ministries and positive activities of other people.

Paul's security did not come in comparing himself with others, in boasting beyond his limits, in taking credit for what others had done, but his security did come from his commitment to the Lord. He boasted in what the Lord had done, and gave Him the credit for it (2 Corinthians 10:17). And he lived out his life with the commitment that the only approval that he would allow to affect his security would be the approval that came from the Lord (2 Corinthians 10:18). That freed him from playing to the applause of his audience. That freed him from doing things purposely to get others' approval because his insecurity needed it. That freed him from vacillating. That freed him from being in the pits when people did not approve of him at any particular time. It freed him from being envious and jealous when other people received more human approval than he did.

When a person grows to the place where he is so conscious of Christ that there is no room for self, then he has become little enough to be really great. Then he has security that is real security indeed. Then he is open enough to be led in a "triumphal procession in Christ" and to be "the fragrance of the knowledge of Him" (2 Corinthians 2:14), and that is to be victorious in the Christian warfare.

Summary

1. Christians are indeed in a warfare.

2. Our characteristics should be that of Christ, including meekness and gentleness.

3. We should not wage war as the world does.

4. The fortresses we take are in people's minds.

5. We wage war according to the divine power—or God's divine nature.

6. The goal of the Christian's warfare is to take thoughts into captivity to obey Christ.

7. The Christian should not use external measurements to determine who is or is not a fellow brother or sister in Christ.

8. Anyone who has authority has it for the purpose of building people up, not tearing them down.

9. We are to be consistent in our proclamation.

10. The power of persuasion is not in the power of our speech, but in the power of the Holy Spirit.

11. We should not depend upon the false security of comparing ourselves with others, boasting beyond limits, or taking credit for what others have done.

12. We should honor people for what they are doing.

13. Our security should rest in the Lord—what He has done, what He is doing, and what He will do.

14. We should live for the commendation of the Lord. That will free us up from being fakes and wishy-washy.

CHAPTER ELEVEN

Defense of Paul's Ministry

2 Corinthians 11

Paul had just spoken against inappropriate boasting (2 Corinthians 10:12-18). But he had not spoken against boasting per se. He admitted that he would boast, but it would be within the proper limits (2 Corinthians 10:8, 13, 14). In 2 Corinthians 11 and 12, we see his boasting within the limits that he had outlined.

All that we read about his boasting in these next two chapters must be understood in light of Paul's concern for the church. He wanted to build people up. He admitted toward the end of the boasting, "Have you been thinking all along that we have been defending ourselves to you? We have been speaking in the sight of God as those in Christ; and everything we do, dear friends, is for your strengthening" (2 Corinthians 12:19).

So Paul's boasting was not for self-advantage, but for the advantage of the church. Apparently, his opponents in the church had been doing such a good job of boasting that Paul realized he had to move into that arena in order to weaken the opponents' position. Nevertheless, Paul still called this boasting activity "foolishness." The fact that he was extremely uncomfortable with it was seen by the number of times he repeated that it was foolish or that he was foolish to do it (2 Corinthians 11:1, 16, 17, 19, 21, 23; 12:6, 11).

After reading all of this, we get the feeling that Paul wished he did not have to go that route. But the Corinthians' reception of those who made that route their method compelled Paul to do so (2 Corinthians 12:11). When Paul asked the people to "put up with a little of my foolishness" (2 Corinthians 11:1), he was talking about their putting up with this boasting. Then he said, "But you are already doing that." He had such confidence that they were his friends that he was sure that they would be patient with him; so he put it in the present tense.

Paul's boasting was about many things: about his jealousy (2 Corinthians 11:2), about his concern for the church (2 Corinthians 11:3, 4), about his apostleship (2 Corinthians 11:5), about his knowledge (2 Corinthians 11:6), about his financial affairs (2 Corinthians 11:7-9), about his love (2 Corinthians 11:10-12), about his status (2 Corinthians 11:16-22), about his service and sufferings (2 Corinthians 11:23-27), and about his anxiety (2 Corinthians 11:28-33).

It is clear that Paul had been pitted against false apostles (2 Corinthians 11:5, 13-15); so Paul outlined some of the characteristics of a true apostle. The implication is that the false apostles were not fulfilling these characteristics. These characteristics also constituted the weapons that Paul used to fight in this battle. Here are some of those apostolic characteristics:

1. A true apostle was uncomfortable with boasting (2 Corinthians 11:1).
2. He cared for the people's progress and their devotion (2 Corinthians 11:2, 3; 12:19).
3. He was concerned for correct teaching and true knowledge (2 Corinthians 11:4, 6).
4. He was humble (2 Corinthians 11:7-10; 12:14).
5. He refused to be detoured from right attitudes and actions (2 Corinthians 11:12).
6. He was willing to call a spade a spade and an error an error (2 Corinthians 11:13-15).
7. He refused to use methods of worldly manipulation (2 Corinthians 11:16-21; 12:16-18).
8. He lived out the role of a suffering-servant leader (2 Corinthians 11:22-33; 12:15).
9. He performed signs, wonders, and miracles (2 Corinthians 12:12).
10. He was concerned about self-conduct (2 Corinthians 12:20-21).

In summary, the true apostle was a suffering servant dedicated to the welfare of the church out of love to God and out of love to God's people. Those are not only characteristic of a true apostle, but also characteristic of any true people helper—something God has called all of us to be.

While we are not to boast or commend ourselves for the purpose of building up ourselves, there may be times when we need to do it so that others will not be deceived by false accusations of false teachers. Our purpose, however, must be to protect others, to build up others, to direct the devotion of others to the Lord and not allow them to be sidetracked. Remember, the only reason Paul was boasting was because false apostles were in the Corinthian church and were confusing them with their many fantastic boasts. Today, there are many people in leadership roles of the church, of para-church organizations, and on television and radio that are making fantastic boasts and are indeed deceiving and manipulating people.

Defense of Paul's Jealousy (11:1-6)

Paul first of all boasted about his jealousy (2 Corinthians 11:2). Jealousy is the talk of lovers. While there is one kind of jealousy that is evil, there is another kind of jealousy that is good and is, in fact, godly. In the Old Testament, God is called a jealous God. The word *jealousy* emphasized a zeal. There is a zeal that is selfish. It is envious. It looks only to self-gratification. It is really selfish passion. It is possessive. It covets another for self-satisfaction only. It raises its head when attention or love is given to someone else. This kind of jealousy always seeks to get and never to give.

There is also a jealousy that is right. Indeed, it safeguards another person. It emerges when those we love are in danger from people who will corrupt their minds and characters. This kind of jealousy is not concerned about prestige, but with the progress of the other person. God's jealousy is seen when His people go after other deities, for God knows that there is no other deity that can save mankind. All other so-called gods are concerned about mankind's destruction, and the devil is the king of that. Man's true happiness and fulfillment and eternity come from having a continuing fellowship with God the Creator of the universe. God knows that, and out of His love for us, He is jealous if we have other gods before Him. As God's jealousy comes from His love, so Paul's jealousy came from genuine love for the welfare of the church. He had connected the people to Christ as a husband to his bride (2 Corinthians 11:2). And Paul wanted the people to be committed to Christ as a "pure virgin" is committed to the bridegroom. That referred to their faithfulness to the Lord. It did not mean that they would never sin, but they would not transfer their allegiance from the Lord Jesus Christ to some other "lord." And that is the danger of the false apostles' teaching.

When Paul said, "I promised you to one husband, to Christ," he was taking on the role of the father of a daughter, a father who loved that daughter enough to have jealous protection for her. Every church leader should have that kind of concern for his congregation. As daughters can be deceived by flamboyant, cheap, imitation lovers, so can the church. The church can be deceived as Eve was (2 Corinthians 11:3). And Paul knew that was going on within the Corinthian congregation at that time. As Paul described the church in the marital situation with Christ, his mind went back to the first marriage—Adam and Eve's—and to Eve's deception. Paul was not concerned that the Corinthians might transfer their love from him to other human beings, but rather that they might transfer their love from Christ to another. He did not want them to be led astray from their sincere and pure devotion to Christ. Isn't it wonderful to see a church leader whose primary concern is the people's "sincere and pure devotion to Christ"? It is easy for human leaders to have a craving for prestige and a love for power, for a following, for being well known, and for advancing in status. When Paul had this concern for his people, he was sharing the same concern of Christ, for Jesus so loves the church as His bride that He desires to "present her to himself as a radiant church, without stain or wrinkle or any other blemish, but holy and blameless" (Ephesians 5:27, 28).

What was causing Paul's fear with the Corinthians? It was that certain people were dumping on the Corinthians a different Jesus, a different spirit, a different gospel, and a different apostle (2 Corinthians 11:4, 5). As Satan gave Eve a different savior (Satan), a different gospel ("It's good for you"), and a different spirit (a demonic one), the false apostles were trying to dump the same thing on the Corinthian church.

The threat to a "sincere" (wholehearted) and "pure" (having no mixed motives) devotion to Christ, is false preaching. And listening to false preaching is the first step in losing our spiritual virginity. In the Old Testament, whenever Israel began to be devoted to another deity, God said they had committed adultery. They had lost spiritual virginity, and that was grounds for spiritual divorce. Whenever we accept Christ, our devotion is to be to Him exclusively. Our main desire should be to serve Him, love Him, obey Him, and respect Him.

But the false apostles were teaching a "Jesus other than the Jesus we preached" (2 Corinthians 11:4). The word for *other* means another of the *same* kind (that is, a similar Jesus, but not the exact Jesus). That is the trickery of Satan. He doesn't major in proclaiming a Jesus who is altogether different from Christ, but a very similar Jesus to the divine Jesus. He has caused many people to believe that Jesus is a good man—but not God. That Jesus is a mere teacher, but not the only perfect teacher. That Jesus is a good social reformer. That Jesus is Lord, but not Lord of *all*. That Jesus may bring salvation, but He is not the *only* way to salvation. However, there is no "other" Jesus. Jesus is unique. Jesus is "one of a kind."

Another Jesus, even slightly different from the Jesus of the Gospels, produces a different spirit. New Testament Christianity is the Christianity of the dispensation of the Holy Spirit. The word for a *different* spirit is the word that means a spirit of an entirely different kind. There is absolutely no similarity between a false spirit and the Holy Spirit. Even a slightly different Jesus produces an entirely different spirit. The differences in a different spirit are seen in the different manifestations of that spirit, the different characteristics of that spirit, and the different destiny of that spirit. The manifestations are counterfeit, the character is less than Christlike, and the destiny is Hell.

If the Lord Jesus Christ of the Gospels is not our Lord, we can house a spirit of materialism rather than the spirit of the Master, a spirit of self and Satan rather than a spirit of the Savior, a spirit of defeatism rather than a spirit of divinity and positiveness, a spirit of the devil rather than a spirit of God.

A different spirit will always produce a different gospel. And again, the word for a *different* gospel means one of an entirely different kind from the good news of God. How is it entirely different? It is not good news of unity with God. It is not good news of unity with man. It is not good news that we become joint heirs with God and Christ. It is not good news of our future in Heaven. It is not good news that in Christ, there is no condemnation. It is not good news that God answers prayer. It is not good news that Jesus Christ is the problem solver. It is not good news that in Christ, there is forgiveness of sins now and forever.

The problem with the Corinthians was that when someone came preaching this other gospel and sounded expert at it, they put up with it and began to cave in to it. So, in a sense, they began to follow a different apostle. So Paul made it clear that he was not inferior to those who claim to be "super-apostles."

Every congregation must take seriously the responsibility to endure sound doctrine and to reject false teaching, even though that false teaching comes from A+ speakers. We cannot permit anyone to teach anything in the name of intellectual freedom because of the power of preaching. Preaching can cause people to follow the preacher.

However, it is interesting that Paul had not demanded that the Corinthians kick out those teachers. There is a time to do that (Titus 3:10), but this particular situation was not one of them. Here, Paul sensed that the greater need was to show them the danger and to defend his position. Unless the Corinthian church would come to Paul's thinking, then any word of excommunication would probably not have been heeded anyway. But if the Corinthians would agree on what Paul was saying in the next two chapters, then a potential excommunication of these false teachers would surely result.

It is always dangerous for immature Christians to evaluate true doctrine by the speaking skills of the leaders. Paul admitted that he was not a "trained speaker" (2 Corinthians 11:6). The word for *trained* is a word that means having received formal training. This was the same kind of charge given against the apostles in Acts 4:13. A "trained speaker" can lead a lot of people down a dangerous path. It is extremely dangerous to say nothing or to say falsehood, but to say it well. It is equally dangerous to listen to someone who is saying nothing or saying falsehood, but saying it well.

Paul openly admitted to some oratorical weakness (1 Corinthians 1:17; 2:4; 2 Corinthians 10:10; 11:6). But men are not saved by the homiletical style of humans, but by the Holy Spirit. Men are not saved by the power of persuasive speech, but rather by the truth. The Holy Spirit blesses truth, not necessarily speaking style. Paul had the one thing going for him that was necessary— true knowledge, and Paul was able to say, in a plain way, "We have made this perfectly clear to you in every way" (2 Corinthians 11:6). While Christian leaders do not have to become flamboyant speakers, Christians need to learn how to communicate in a way that people can clearly understand the message. Jesus was a master at using one-syllable words and at using illustrations that small children could understand. No wonder the crowds flocked to Him. And no wonder He spoke as someone who had authority. The one who really has authority is the one who can translate complex truth into simple statements.

Paul's knowledge came from Jesus (2 Corinthians 12:1-6). And that source is quite enough.

Defense of Paul's Financial Policy (11:7-12)

When Paul asked the question, "Was it a sin for me to lower myself . . . by preaching the gospel of God to you free of charge?" he was not suggesting that it was a moral wrong. The word for *sin* means to miss the mark. Did Paul miss the mark of relating to the Corinthians by not receiving pay? Did he offend them by refusing an honorarium? That sounds like an odd question to ask in today's world, but it was the right question in that time. Speakers who refused to receive an income were considered to be cheap imitators of quality. As a matter of fact, the greater the insight speakers had, then the greater the fee they charged. From that perspective, Paul should have asked for top billing. But to be a "free" speaker in that day was looked down upon. We have a tendency to do that today. Have you ever noticed a street-corner preacher? He may be sincere, but he is not usually taken very seriously.

In that day, the Sophists taught that if a teacher was paid nothing, his teaching was worth nothing. Paul's opponents may have been using this argument, saying that since Paul took nothing, his teaching was worth nothing. His lack of taking support alone would be proof that he was an inferior teacher. It showed that he was a maverick. His opponents may have been saying, "Paul is a free-lance speaker. He is autonomous and thus not responsible to anyone. He is simply speaking his own words for his own self-gratification. Some people get stroked by having crowds, and that is Paul's problem." But Paul countered all of that kind of possible opposition. Paul made it clear that he did not speak for money. The only reason that he spoke was to serve other people.

Paul was not opposed to receiving money. In fact, he did receive "support" from other churches (2 Corinthians 11:8). The word for *support* is a Greek word that was used for paying military people their food rations. Paul received enough to get by on in Corinth. Paul did not want his new converts to think he was sponging off them. He did not want to be a "burden" to them. The word for *burden* was a medical term for numbing someone prior to potentially hurting them with surgery or by some other means. The word then began to be used for making the kind of overcharges to people that really stings. Why would Paul have used a term like this? Perhaps it was because he realized that a person could not really evaluate the worth of a person's preaching until after conversion. So any money he might have taken might have numbed them and thus blocked their acceptance of the gospel. So his love for them considered this possible blockage. Evidently, he did not consider the backlash that would come from it. Some churches today have so understood that non-Christians cannot appreciate the value of preaching that they tell the visitors at offering time to not give to the offering.

But Paul really wanted to continue his preaching to the Corinthians without money from them. He said he would "continue to do so" (2 Corinthians 11:9). This was not because Paul did not believe that preachers should be paid for their preaching. On the contrary, he wrote elsewhere that God expects the church to take care of its preachers (1 Corinthians 9). But Paul's personal policy while in Corinth and while ministering to the Corinthians was to receive no monies from them. It was not because he did not love them, but rather because he did love them (2 Corinthians 11:11). In fact, he did it in order to "cut the ground from under those who want an opportunity to be considered equal with us in the things they boast about" (2 Corinthians 11:12).

Paul knew the kind of opposition he was up against in Corinth. And he knew that none of the false apostles would have such concern for the Corinthians that they would do what he had done without lining their pockets. Paul's refusal to take income should not be seen as an excuse for not paying preachers. It was a refusal for that time in that situation in order to disarm the false preachers. Paul would not permit himself to be compared with those false preachers in any way. Here are several things about those false preachers that disgusted Paul:

1. They did not have the same knowledge (2 Corinthians 11:6).
2. They preyed upon the people and enslaved them (2 Corinthians 11:20).
3. They put on airs (2 Corinthians 11:20).
4. They peddled the Word (2 Corinthians 2:17).
5. They were not true apostles (2 Corinthians 11:13, 14).
6. They were not suffering servants (2 Corinthians 11:22-29).
7. They lined their pockets with their preaching (2 Corinthians 11:7-12).
8. They were deceitful, disguising themselves and pretending to be what they were not (2 Corinthians 11:13, 14).

When we see all of the differences above, then we can better understand why Paul would not accept any pay at Corinth. He did not want to do *anything* that they were doing lest some people would confuse him with them.

The Unveiling of False Apostles (11:13, 14)

Not everyone who claims to be one of God's leaders is. That was a problem in Paul's day just as it is a problem today. In 2 Corinthians 11:13, 14, Paul listed several characteristics of the false apostles who were deceiving some of the Corinthians:

1. They were deceitful workmen.
2. They masqueraded.
3. They were servants of the devil.
4. Their end would be destruction.

The word for *deceitful* is the word for baiting a hook. These false apostles lured people to their position by the way they spoke. They sounded so smooth, but people did not see the hook that was inside. They also disguised themselves by pretending to be what they were not. The word for *masquerading* is a Greek word that means changing the outer form. It describes someone who changed externally for people to see, but not internally. They had a good cover-up. They were wolves in sheep's clothing. They claimed to be gentlemen of the cloth, but were nothing but cloth. They were so good at masquerading that they appeared to be "servants of righteousness," but that should not surprise us. Satan himself masquerades as an "angel of light." The word for *serpent* in Genesis 3 is a Hebrew word that can also mean brightness. Satan masqueraded himself as an "angel of light" as far back as the Garden of Eden. And he continues to do it through human beings today.

Defense of Paul's Boasting (11:16-21)

In the midst of this writing, Paul communicated his discomfort with boasting. In fact, he admitted that he was taking the stance of a "fool" in doing it. But he sensed the need to do it because the Corinthians had forced him to (2 Corinthians 12:11) by listening to the boasting of the false apostles who came as "super-apostles." Paul rebuked the Corinthians for putting up with those "fools" when they were "so wise." After all, anyone can listen to fools. It is a shame when the sensible are duped by the senseless; when the wise are led astray by the foolish.

Paul then described some of the activities of these false teachers:

1. They were involved in tyranny. They enslaved their hearers. They caused their hearers to be in bondage to them. What powerful speakers they must have been! And this still goes on today.
2. They were involved in exploitation. They preyed upon their people, rather than praying for them.
3. They took their people in ("takes advantage of you").
4. They exalted themselves by putting on airs ("pushes himself forward").
5. They insulted their audience ("slaps you in the face"). Slapping in the face was one of the lowest forms of insulting someone in that day.

Too many religious leaders have people under their control today. They have done precisely that for which Paul condemned the false apostles.

Instead of mistreating his people, Paul chose to love them. Instead of enslaving them, he chose to serve them. Instead of exploiting them, he chose to encourage them. Instead of taking advantage of them, he was willing to be taken advantage of by them. Instead of pushing himself forward, he wanted to build them up. Instead of insulting them, he wanted to inspire them. If Paul's position was seen as a "weak position," then Paul admitted to that weakness (2 Corinthians 11:21). Preachers, elders, Sunday-school teachers, college professors, and all other leaders need to re-read this section carefully and commit themselves to being Christ's kind of leaders. If you want to be an understudy of a great leader, then go to the top of the list. Become an understudy of Christ and Paul. Time has vindicated their tactics. Don't go the route of cheap imitators. Too many Christian leaders are going that route now because it gives instant success. A person can sell either soap or the Savior by applying the hard-handed methods of temporary marketing. But if we do that in religion, all we have sold is soap, which washes away. We have not proclaimed the Savior who saves. Each leader must ask, "What is making the sales? Is it my method or the truth of the content?" There is something wrong when the church does not grow because of preaching, but then catches on fire with cheap substitutes.

Paul was willing to be seen as "weak" in comparison to the super powerful and great false apostles who used the secular methods to enslave their audiences. The question is, how are we willing to be seen? While Jesus emptied himself and took on the form of a servant (Philippians 2), it is easy for many leaders to fill themselves and take on the form of a human lord.

Paul's Sufferings (11:22-29)

Evidently, the false apostles had been pushing their status and services. So Paul picked that up. If they wanted to talk about *status,* Paul had it (2 Corinthians 11:22). If they wanted to talk about *services,* Paul was outstanding (2 Corinthians 11:23). If they wanted to talk about *suffering,* no one had suffered the way Paul had (2 Corinthians 11:23-28). If they wanted to talk about *sensitivity,* Paul excelled in having concern for the right things— for all the churches (2 Corinthians 11:29).

Paul had the correct status. He was not just a Jew, but a "Hebrew." That referred to a Jew who still spoke Aramaic. He had not lost his native language, as many liberal Jews had done. He was also a Jew who was an Israelite, a member of God's covenant people. He was also from the correct family, "the seed of Abraham," which was an heir to the promise.

If they wanted to talk about being a servant, Paul was a servant to the correct person—to Christ. The word for *servant* (2 Corinthians 11:23) is the word for one who performed lowly service. Paul was willing to be a suffering servant, and we can see that in what follows. Paul was willing to wear his pains like decorations. His crosses made up his crown. Here is a listing of those suffering-servant activities:

1. He had "worked much harder." That refers to being terribly fatigued.
2. He had "been in prison more frequently." Up to the time that Paul wrote this, we know of only one time he was in prison (in Philippi, Acts 16). But Paul's confession here lets us know that what we read in the book of Acts is just the tip of the iceberg of all the problems that Paul had encountered through those days.
3. He had "been flogged more severely." Literally, the Greek says "times without number." He could not even count the number of times that he had been beaten. He did remember two different kinds of beatings and the amount of those, but beyond that he was not able to count. (See verses 24, 25.)

4. He had "been exposed to death again and again." Several times Paul was left for dead and, in fact, would not have been left had people not thought that he had actually died.

5. "Five times [he] received from the Jews the forty lashes minus one." Forty lashes was the limit of Jewish beating. The penalty for exceeding the limit was so severe that those who administered the punishment regularly stopped short by one to be sure they did not accidentally exceed forty.

6. "Three times [he] was beaten with rods." We read of only one beating in Acts (16:22, 23), and there we don't know whether it was with a rod or a whip. So again, we know that Acts is just giving us the tip of the iceberg of Paul's difficulties. Remember that Paul still had several years left to live after Acts was written.

7. "Once . . . stoned." A stoning was calculated to kill a person. In the usual Jewish stoning, a five-foot hole was dug and the person was thrown into the hole face first. The accuser picked up the first boulder and threw it on the person. The first stone was usually selected to be large enough to break the person's back. Other people piled stones on the person until they thought he was dead.

   The report of Paul's stoning in Lystra does not seem to be consistent with this method; so without more information, we're not entirely sure the stoning he mentions here is the same one as recorded in Acts 14 or another not recorded elsewhere.

8. "Three times . . . shipwrecked." Paul "spent a night and a day in the open sea" waiting for rescue. (And all three shipwrecks mentioned here were before the one mentioned in Acts 27!)

9. He was "constantly on the move."

10. He was "in danger from rivers."

11. He was "in danger from bandits."

12. He was "in danger from [his] own countrymen."

13. He was "in danger from the Gentiles."

14. He was "in danger in the city."

15. He was "in danger in the country."

16. He was "in danger at sea."

17. He was "in danger from false brothers."

18. He was often fatigued, "labored and toiled."

19. He had "often gone without sleep."

20. He had been hungry.
21. He had been thirsty.
22. He had "often gone without food."
23. He had been "cold and naked."

Look at the above list again. Being a Christian does not always mean that every day is going to be sweeter than the day before. The song "Every Day With Jesus Is Sweeter Than the Day Before" is not one that Paul could have sung if he felt that all the external circumstances would get better and better and better. No matter where Paul was, he was in danger. When he was in the city or in the country; when he was on the land or in the sea; when he was with his kinfolk or with foreigners, he never got away from danger because he never got away from his devotion to Christ. That devotion for Christ caused Paul to speak out for Christ. If Paul had just shut up, played religion, stayed in the closet, and conformed to his environment, he would never have experienced the above difficulties.

Now what false apostles are willing to go through all of that? It is not enough to listen to how well a man puts words together. Sometimes that man needs to show how he has put his life on the line for the Lord. Perhaps a mark of a true servant would be to give away his jet plane to feed the hungry, to live in a smaller house to help fund a mission cause, or to buy clothes from a department store instead of a custom tailor to help clothe the naked.

Besides all the external pressures, Paul's integrity as a servant of Christ was seen by his internal pressure of having concern for *all* the churches (2 Corinthians 11:28). Paul shared empathy with people. He knew what it meant to feel weak. He knew what it meant to be led into sin. When he said "Who is led into sin, and I do not inwardly burn?" (2 Corinthians 11:29), he was probably referring to the fact that he knew what it was to be tempted with sexual sins throughout all of his travel. The word for *burn* is the word that Paul used in 1 Corinthians 7:9 when he talked about a single person's burning with passion for another. Would that surprise us to hear that Paul knew what is was to be tempted? Would that surprise us to hear that Paul knew what it meant to be a male in his sexuality? Paul knew what it meant for the church to be misled in a false teaching because he had been misled before the road to Damascus. And Paul knew what it meant for people to go through difficult temptation in which they were "weak" because

Paul had gone through that. He admitted in Romans 7 that the things he would not do he found himself doing, and the things he wanted to do, he found he did not do. Paul was a great leader partly because he had not lost contact with what it meant to be human.

Conclusion (11:30-33)

While his opponents boasted in their strength, Paul boasted in his weaknesses. By doing that, he continually kept his faith in the Lord.

Paul brought up one episode that showed his humiliation. That was the time that he had to leave Damascus in a basket. That was a humiliating time for Paul, but it happened because Paul had the boldness to stand up for the Lord. Paul had begun to evangelize in Damascus after he became a Christian. Some people feel that was too early, but remember, Paul was a Hebrew of Hebrews. He had advanced in Judaism above all of his equals. He knew what it meant for the Messiah to come. And when he was convinced that Jesus was the Messiah, he had the maturity to proclaim that message.

Immediately after Paul evangelized in Damascus, he went into Arabia, where he stayed for three years (Galatians 1). What did he do in Arabia? He received instructions from the Lord, but I am convinced he also evangelized. In fact, I am convinced that he evangelized so effectively that he encountered opposition in Arabia as he did in many other places. After he spent time in Arabia, he came back into Damascus, but he probably came back into Damascus "on the run;" for King Aretas, who was king over the Arabian area, was after Paul. That king had the city of Damascus staked out for Paul. So the apostle, who had correct understanding, who had been converted by Jesus himself on the road to Damascus, who had received special revelation from the Lord in Arabia, who was proclaiming Jesus in response to Jesus' own commission, was in a "weak" situation in Damascus. His life was threatened. He was a fugitive on the run, and he had to leave at night in a basket let over a wall. He was willing to be a "basket case" for Jesus.

Summary

1. Christians, especially Christian leaders, should have correct concern for the church's devotion to Jesus.

2. There is no other Jesus, no other Spirit, and no other gospel than the ones in the New Testament.

3. The church is built upon the foundation of the New Testament apostles. We should not be open to new apostles today.

4. Satan masquerades himself as an angel of light.

5. Satan's servants masquerade themselves as servants of righteousness.

6. False teachers will enslave, exploit, take advantage of, and insult others, while they exalt themselves.

7. The sincere servant of the Lord is willing to be fatigued, mistreated, endangered, and deprived for the sake of his ministry.

8. The true servant of the Lord has daily anxiety for all the churches.

9. The true servant of the Lord knows what it is to be weak and to burn inwardly with temptation.

10. The true servant of the Lord knows what it means to be humiliated. He is not always on top of everything.

CHAPTER TWELVE

Defense of Paul's Apostleship

2 Corinthians 12

Paul continued his uncomfortable boasting by including the most uncomfortable experience of all—an ecstatic experience. This was probably uncomfortable for Paul for many reasons:
1. It might cause the ones who read about it to think that Paul was superior to them, or to believe he was claiming to be superior.
2. It could cause people to wonder why they had not received a similar experience.
3. It is the kind of experience that cannot be verified.
4. Many people in the first century were evidently trying to boost themselves by claiming various kinds of ecstatic experiences; so Paul was uncomfortable in joining that bandwagon. In fact, Paul was so uncomfortable with it that he nearly camouflaged the identity of the one who had the experience. A person has to read carefully to note that Paul was speaking about himself.

This is the only time we hear Paul speaking of this kind of experience except for the experience on the road to Damascus. Although Luke recorded some visions that Paul had, and some miraculous interventions of God, Paul himself did not talk about those experiences. But evidently, Paul's opponents had boasted of similar experiences and used that as a way to get a following. So Paul felt the need to let his Corinthian brothers and sisters know that he himself had also had supernatural experiences. But there were at least two important differences. First, the false apostles talked a lot about them, Paul did not. And second, the false apostles evidently used those experiences to build themselves up; Paul did not. In fact, we would never know about it in Paul's life had it not been for those who built themselves up by it. The same thing is true about Paul's speaking in tongues. We would never have known that Paul spoke in tongues had it not been for one notation written to people who were using the experience in competitive ways (1 Corinthians 14:18).

Visions and Revelations for an Apostle (12:1-6)

When Paul said "I must" (2 Corinthians 12:1), he was talking about the necessity caused by the situation at hand. When Paul said, "There is nothing to be gained," he was referring to personal gain to himself. The boasting did not mean that he was a better apostle. The boasting did not mean that he would receive more financial income. The boasting did not mean that he would have a better self-image. It did not even mean that it would cause the Corinthians to become better people. As a matter of fact, they had changed through repentance prior to knowing about this ecstatic experience. It was the power of the Holy Spirit through the letters that Paul wrote and through the persons who ministered in Corinth that caused them to change. Paul's boasting was not to receive gain for himself, but rather to counter some claims of the false apostles who were taking advantage of some of the Corinthians.

Up to this time, Paul's boasting had emphasized his zeal for the church, his concern about the Corinthians' devotion to the Lord, his financial policy, his failure to manipulate and take advantage of people, and his willingness to suffer for the benefit of others. But now Paul went on to "visions and revelations from the Lord." These were divine encounters. *Visions* refers to what Paul saw. *Revelations* refers to what Paul heard, and both of those came directly from the Lord. The "man in Christ" to whom this happened was Paul himself. He made that clear in 2 Corinthians 12:7, "To keep me from becoming conceited because of these surpassingly great revelations, there was given me a thorn in my flesh, a messenger of Satan, to torment me."

Paul remembered precisely when the experience happened, fourteen years before the time of this writing. However, we are not able to pinpoint precisely where Paul was at that time. We know generally what happened, but not how it happened. Generally, Paul was "caught up to the third heaven."

The phrase *third heaven* was a Jewish way of describing the location of God's presence. The first heaven referred to our atmosphere—the air we breathe here on earth. The second heaven referred to what we see above our air where the stars are located, and the third heaven is the presence of God. When Jesus ascended to the Father after His resurrection, He went "through the heavens" (Hebrews 4:14). That is, He went through the first and second heavens. The Greek word for *caught up* is used only here and in 1 Thessalonians 4:17. In both places, it refers to a personal meeting with the Lord.

Paul further identified the "third heaven" as "paradise" (2 Corinthians 12:4). Paradise is the place of the righteous departed. The word was first of all used to describe a park of a king or of a nobility. The Garden of Eden was called by this name. In paradise, the quality of life in the Garden of Eden will be restored. Jesus told the thief on the cross that he would be with Him in paradise (Luke 23:43). Wherever paradise is, Jesus is there. That's what makes it paradise.

This was such an ecstatic experience for Paul that he did not know how it happened. Did he go in his bodily form, or did he go outside his bodily form? It was written in a non-Biblical source that Enoch paid a bodily visit to the Heavenly throne and returned (1 Enoch 12:1ff, 17:1ff). There are many pieces of Jewish literature that talk about a person who left his body when he went on a journey by way of visions and received special instructions from the Lord. But Paul did not know the how of it, nor was he trying to establish a special methodology for others to follow.

Paul's attitude was an attitude to be copied, "I do not know— God knows" (2 Corinthians 12:2, 3). More leaders need to be able to admit that we do not know how God does what He does. Too many times we get hooked on the method rather than the Master.

There was another attitude of Paul that deserves modeling. This was evidently the first time in fourteen years that Paul had shared with anyone this experience. Paul never saw himself as having been called to preach about visions and revelations he had received. He was called to preach the crucified Christ. He did not gain his popularity by calling special attention to his supernatural encounters with God. Whatever acceptance he received, he received by communicating what God had done in Christ. Paul wanted people to receive what God had done in the death and resurrection of Jesus, not by trying to duplicate supernatural experiences for individuals.

Whatever Paul heard in paradise, he was not permitted to tell. It is possible that God shared with him truths that God chose not to put within the pages of the Bible. If that is the case, then this suggests to us that no one has the right to claim extra-Biblical revelation that adds content to the Bible. The completed Bible is enough for us. And as soon as we begin to listen to anyone who claims to have extra insight because of special visions and revelations, we had better not listen. For if God did not permit Paul to share what he heard, God will not permit anyone to share extra-Biblical content. It is to Paul's merit that he did not even give a hint as to what the content might have been.

Paul made it clear that his boasting had nothing to do with his own doing: "I will boast about a man like that, but I will not boast about myself" (2 Corinthians 12:5). The experiences did not happen because of Paul's own merit. He mentioned the experience, but made nothing of it before others that would benefit himself in their eyes. He would not say, "Look how great I am! Look how close to the Lord I live! If you want all God has, have a vision like I have had! If you really want to hear what the Lord has to say, then listen to me, for I have received special revelation from Him." Paul did not make people feel inferior because they had not gone through similar experiences, nor did he think that he had superiority over them because of those experiences. It is very clear that Paul would not use such experiences for the purpose of getting a following for himself.

All Paul had to boast about in himself was his weaknesses. From his perspective, he deserved the weaknesses, not the visions and revelations. A person is not a mature disciple because he has visions, revelations, or any other ecstatic experiences. The mark of a mature disciple is seen in his attitude with those experiences, not just the experiences themselves. The mature disciple is one who can love others as Jesus does (John 13:34, 35). A true disciple is one who carries the marks of 1 Corinthians 13:4-7, not necessarily all of the experiences listed in 1 Corinthians 12.

When Paul boasted of his weaknesses, then he really exalted the Lord, who ministered to him and through him in spite of those weaknesses.

Paul did not want anyone to think more of him than what they could observe him doing and could hear him saying (2 Corinthians 12:6). He was not going to exploit them by suggesting that something special was happening inside of him that they could not see or hear themselves. He would not even say, "The Lord is giving me special knowledge, and here is what that knowledge is. . . ." Some people, when in front of large audiences, will interrupt their sermons with something like this, "What's that, Lord? What are you saying to me, Lord? Oh! Okay, Lord, I've got it!" Then that person will share with his audience a special revelation that God has supposedly just given to him. Paul would have nothing to do with that kind of showmanship. If God did speak to someone, then let that someone praise the Lord; but not sell it to others and not use it in such a public display that would cause people to want to follow that person more. Paul refused to allow others to evaluate him based on his mystical experiences, but rather by his empirical, objective, show-and-tell realities. Paul would not market his experiences. And yet, Paul was living in a time when people were very open to the subjective. And we are living in a similar time today. The tragedy is that many are taking advantage of people's openness and gullibility.

Paul's Power (12:7-10)

Paul knew firsthand the strong temptation to be self-elated over special supernatural experiences. He might have blown himself out of proportion had God not allowed Satan to give Paul a "thorn in my flesh." Paul accepted his thorn in the flesh as a moral governor for him—as a disciplinarian to keep him from being conceited. Paul also saw this thorn in his flesh as a "messenger of Satan."

What was that thorn in his flesh? As Paul did not reveal the content of the visions and revelations, he did not reveal the identity of the thorn in his flesh. As he would not prey upon peoples' emotions over special visions and revelations, so he would not prey upon their sympathy over his thorn in the flesh. But Paul sensed that he needed that thorn in his flesh to be a continual reminder to him of his weaknesses and that whatever positive events happened through his life happened because of God in his life and not because of his own superiority. Paul was then freer to give God the credit. The moment we elevate self, we dethrone God. John the Baptist got at this when he said, "He must become greater; I must become less" (John 3:30). When John's disciples heard John speak, they followed Jesus (John 1:35-37). That was the attitude of the apostle Paul. And that is to be the attitude of any mature disciple.

In speculating about the identity of the thorn in his flesh, scholars have suggested many possibilities. We might group them in four possible categories. First, it might have been some kind of sickness of the flesh. Various scholars have identified this as malaria, partial blindness, epilepsy, insomnia, and severe migraine headaches. If that is the case, then the "weakness" referred to a physical weakness.

Second, it might have been a temptation of the flesh. I prefer this understanding. It seems to fit the broader context better. Paul spoke about feeling "weak" in 2 Corinthians 11:29. There he was speaking about people who were led into sin. He also confessed that when people were led into sin, he understood it, because he too felt weak and he inwardly burned. We have already seen that the Greek word for *burn* was a word that Paul used before to refer to burning with sexual passion (1 Corinthians 7:9). To understand this thorn in the flesh as a recurring temptation also better explains how Paul saw that thorn in his flesh as a "messenger of Satan, to torment me." Satan is a master tempter. Paul was not only a disciple of the Lord, but also a male in the midst of a world filled with sexual promiscuity. It may be that Paul knew what it meant to be often sexually tempted. But being aware of that also would have made him aware of the fact that he was human, he was vulnerable, he was fragile, and he needed to depend upon the presence and power of the Lord. If this was the thorn in his flesh, then Paul was speaking out of personal experience as well as inspiration when he wrote 1 Corinthians 10:13, "No temptation has seized you except what is common to man. And God is faithful; he will not let you be tempted beyond what you can bear. But when you are tempted, he will also provide a way out so that you can stand up under it."

Third, the thorn in his flesh could have referred to his anxiety over the churches (2 Corinthians 11:38). And finally, the thorn in his flesh may also have referred to the persecutions and hardships that he experienced in life. When the Lord refused to remove the thorn in his flesh, Paul determined rather to "delight in weaknesses, in insults, in hardships, in persecutions, in difficulties" (2 Corinthians 12:10). That fits the context of what Paul just moved out of in 2 Corinthians 11:23-33.

The truth is, we do not know what it was, but we know from whom it came—Satan. And we know who allowed it—God. And we know why—to help keep Paul humble. Satan tests us for the purpose of destroying us, but God allows it to happen for the purpose of maturing us (1 Peter 1:6, 7; Romans 5:1-5).

192

If Paul needed a reminder of his humanness and weakness, so do we. It is through the thorns in our flesh that we can be reminded that God's treasure is indeed in "jars of clay," which are breakable, vulnerable, and fragile. And that treasure is in weak vessels in order to show that the "all surpassing power is from God and not from us" (2 Corinthians 4:7). So it was with Paul. Although Paul prayed three times to God to take that thorn in his flesh away, God replied, "My grace is sufficient for you, for my power is made perfect in weakness" (2 Corinthians 12:9). So Paul moved from despising the weakness to delighting in it. For when Paul recognized his humanness, then he was more open to depend upon the presence of the Lord. He moved from a prayer to send it away to a praise for its presence.

While we cannot objectively pinpoint what the thorn in his flesh was, we can conclude that in no way did that thorn weaken Paul's faith in the Lord. It never caused Paul to doubt his self-worth or to say, "What have I done to deserve this? A good Christian is free from difficulties. Every problem a Christian has is a direct retribution to sin in his life; so what have I done wrong?"

It is clear that Paul had weaknesses of humanity and was also filled with the power of God. Just look at how that power was manifested in the way he traveled, the way he wrote, how he reacted to opposition, how he reacted to slander, how he did not quit in the midst of persecutions, and how he handled team members who deserted him. Paul was able to accomplish much for God because he tapped into the power of God while recognizing his own weaknesses.

Are we prone to criticize someone if he gets much done for God? It is the person who is accomplishing much that often gets shot down by jealous and envious peers. We are too quick to think that person is doing a lot because he is trying to tap into prestige, though perhaps all he has done is to tap into the power of God. Our smallness is often seen by how we attack someone else's bigness. Our smallness in misunderstandings is also seen in how we attack someone else's weakness.

Paul's Signs (12:11-13)

Paul never put much emphasis on the miraculous. He mentioned the miraculous here and in Galatians 3:5; Romans 15:19; Hebrews 2:4; and in 1 Corinthians. But, the "super-apostles" had forced Paul to remind the Corinthians that the marks of a true apostle—signs, wonders, and miracles—were done among them. In the early history of the church, miracles were done by the apostles (Acts 2:43). However, they were not done by *only* the apostles, for Paul spoke about God's giving members in the church of Corinth various gifts, some of which were gifts to do miracles. However, a true apostle was authenticated by God partly by the ability to do signs, wonders, and miracles. That's one way that God spotlighted who His inspired spokesmen were over against who the false apostles were. There were many people in the first century who claimed to have a word of the Lord; so God credentialed His inspired spokesmen (Hebrews 2:1-4).

A *sign* was a divine activity that pointed beyond itself to someone else. A person is never to worship the sign, but rather allow his life to be pointed in the direction of that sign. God gave Moses the ability to do signs so that people would know that Moses was their leader. The people did not ask to repeat the signs, but were expected to follow Moses. A *wonder* is the people's reaction to seeing that sign. They were amazed. The word *miracle* is the Greek word that literally means power. While *wonder* refers to the reaction of the people, *power* refers to the source—from God. These signs were not just humanly designed, but divinely empowered.

Paul reminded the Corinthians that they had observed those miraculous interventions; so they were not behind other churches in that. The only way he may have treated them in an "inferior" way was that he was never a financial burden to them (2 Corinthians 12:13). And if they saw that as a problem, then Paul asked for their forgiveness. In asking for forgiveness, Paul showed another mark of a mature disciple. No one is too great to ask others for forgiveness. No one is too great to admit, "I have wronged you!" We do not have to wait until we have actually sinned against someone to ask for their forgiveness. We need to ask for forgiveness when we are aware that we have offended someone, even though our action was not a moral sin. In that way, we help to tighten up the unity and fellowship within God's family. Paul evidently did not consider it a sin not to receive financial payment from them. Rather, it was wrong for him not to have explained the reason behind it. So Paul immediately made it clear that the next time he came, he would still not be a financial burden to them. That teaches us that we need to practice clear communication with people so they can have an understanding for the reasons and motives of our activities. It is so easy to misread, misjudge, and jump to false conclusions when all we see are the activities. When we communicate clearly our reasons, then our activities are more easily acceptable. While we may be right in an activity, we may be wrong in not communicating our reasons for that activity.

Paul's Continual Commitment to Others (12:14-18)

Here Paul explained his reasons for not having been a financial burden to the Corinthians. It was not because he did not consider his students to be valuable enough to receive money from, but rather because he did not want them to think that he was interested in their possessions. He was not interested in their savings, but rather in their souls. So he was not treating them as a traveling teacher treats his paying students; rather, he was treating them as a parent treats a child. Children do not have to pay for all of the services they receive from the parents. If that were the case, every parent today would be a millionaire.

The heartbeat of a mature, unselfish disciple is seen in 2 Corinthians 12:15: "So I will very gladly spend for you everything I have and expend myself as well." That sentence should be burned into the heart of every disciple of Jesus. That is the core of a servant's attitude. That is the motivation of a servant's activities. That attitude will cause servants not to be disturbed when they are called in the middle of the night. It will cause disciples not to be upset when someone wants them to go the second mile. That attitude will cause people of status not to feel that they are above doing ordinary, menial tasks for the benefit of others. To say, "I will spend and be spent," requires a Christlike attitude. It describes in a beautiful way the central characteristic of God. "I will spend" refers to economics. "I will be spent" refers to energy. To say, "I will spend and be spent," is to say, "All that I have and all that I am is available for God's use for the benefit of others." The one who says that is a real people helper.

In verse 16, Paul corrected another misconception that some of the Corinthians had. Evidently, some of the opponents had suggested that Paul did not take pay in order to win their confidence, but later would exploit them after he had them won. When Paul used the words *crafty fellow* and *caught you by trickery,* he was probably using words that had been charged against him. The idea was, "Guess what's going to happen when Paul puts you on his mailing list? He'll send you his personal bill then. And he will send his personal collection agents to get a big offering. It will not stop." Aren't there preachers who are doing that today? They will tell you that you can send for something free, but then you continually get an emotional appeal for that "bill" the rest of your life because you are on their mailing list. So Paul corrected that possible charge against him by making it clear that none of the people he sent to them exploited them. The people Paul had sent to them acted with the same kind of conduct with which Paul had acted when he was with them. So he was not "a crafty fellow," nor did he catch them "by trickery." The word *trickery* is a form of the same Greek word that Paul used earlier of the "*deceitful* workmen," and refers to baiting a hook. That's what the false apostles had been doing, but Paul never once baited any hook.

Paul's Boasting (12:19-21)

Now we see why Paul moved into boasting. It was not to defend himself, as the false apostles had used boasting, but rather to strengthen the Corinthians. The way boasting strengthened the Corinthians was to let them see that Paul was not inferior to these other so-called apostles.

As long as some continued to think that false apostles were above Paul, then that could be the seed for in-house quarreling, jealousy, outbursts of anger, factions, slander, gossip, arrogance, and disorder (2 Corinthians 12:20). And as that continued to grow, immorality would grow in the church. That was why Paul mentioned the fact that some might not repent of "impurity, sexual sin and debauchery." When fellowship is broken, then sensual living can be expected to follow. The three words for sexual immorality show a progression in seriousness. *Impurity* refers to being not pure. *Sexual sin* is from a Greek word that refers to every kind of unlawful sexual perversion. So the impurity was multiplying in many different kinds of expressions. *Debauchery* refers to unrestrained behavior, when people are not embarrassed by what they are doing. They do not care who knows and they do not care who sees. *Debauchery* refers to willful defiance of public expectations. A person who is at the state of debauchery is a person who is totally insensitive to both immorality and public decency.

It is a shame that this kind of activity can happen inside a Christian church. But the seed for its happening is planted when

God's people take their eyes off Jesus Christ and turn their eyes onto false teachers. It can happen when there is in-house fighting that causes people to turn their energy from the Savior to self. In-house fighting is escalated when people divide up over which teaching is false and which teaching is true. So Paul spent three chapters reminding the Corinthians of who he was, what he was like, what he had gone through, and how God had authenticated him. All of that was for the purpose of strengthening the Corinthians' commitment to the Lord and their fellowship with one another so their life-style could reflect who they really were—disciples of Jesus.

Summary

1. We are not to take selfish advantage of our spiritual experiences.

2. In many ways we need to be reminded of our humanness, vulnerability, and weakness. A thorn in our flesh can do that.

3. God's power fills our weaknesses.

4. False apostles try to imitate and counterfeit true apostles.

5. True apostles in the first century were authenticated by signs, wonders, and miracles.

6. We need to communicate clearly the motives for our actions lest we be misunderstood.

7. We need to be willing to spend and be spent for the benefit of others.

8. Whatever we do, we need to do it for the building up of others.

9. We need to speak and live in such a way that people's priorities and attentions are turned to the Lord.

10. In-house fightings and factions can lead to an increase of immorality by members of a fellowship.

11. We need to found our faith upon what the New Testament apostles and prophets have written, and not be vulnerable to self-made apostles and prophets today.

CHAPTER THIRTEEN

Readiness for Paul's Third Visit

2 Corinthians 13

A Warning (13:1-4)

While some people charged that Paul was "timid" when face to face with them, but "bold" when away (2 Corinthians 10:1), Paul repeated something that he told them during his second visit—he was going to exercise stern discipline for those who had not repented of their previous wrongs. But his action would not be out of unsupported haste. "Every matter must be established by the testimony of two or three witnesses" (2 Corinthians 13:1). That reference has two possible meanings:

1. When Paul arrived, he would demand two or three witnesses for any loose charges that had been made either against him or against others. That demand would protect some and pester others. He would not be moved by emotionalism to make snappy decisions.

2. The "two or three witnesses" may refer to Paul's second and upcoming third visit. That is, he himself will have witnessed two or three times the wrongs that some of them had been engaged in. And if they had not changed after Paul's third on-the-scene witness, he would execute stern discipline.

Number 2 above seems to fit the immediate context. Paul had evidently observed for the second time how some of them had not repented when he visited them on his second visit and warned them to get their act together before his next visit. When Paul said, "I will not spare those who sinned earlier" (2 Corinthians 13:2), he was referring to those who had been involved in immoral practices for a while and had not repented even though they had received corrective teaching. "Not sparing" them is the talk of a parent disciplining a child. "Any of the others" refers to those Corinthians who had recently been influenced by the false apostles and were caving in to the life-style of a non-Christian.

Evidently, some of the Corinthians had urged Paul to act sternly as proof that he was an apostle and that Christ was speaking through him. The argument they used must have been something like this: "Christ is powerful. If Christ is in Paul and Paul represents Christ, then Paul needs to show more power." But Paul showed that even Christ's power came after people observed His "weakness" (2 Corinthians 13:4). The Corinthians had evidently forgotten that a mark of Christ's maturity and a mark of His power under control was that Jesus did not retaliate and was not too quick to be aggressive. In fact, Jesus allowed people to crucify Him. That's what many people consider to be weakness.

What is "weak" according to man's estimation is really a demonstration of power according to God's estimation. So while people interpreted that Christ was crucified "in weakness," He really lived and continues to live by God's power. And since Paul was in Christ, then Paul could admit that he was "weak in Him." Paul was speaking here about being "weak" according to man's estimation. As a result of Paul's linkage with Christ, he would not act hastily to punish people who had disobeyed God, and/or hurt Paul. If Christ could keep His self-control while being nailed to the cross, then Paul could keep his self-control while being misunderstood, slandered, belittled, and verbally crucified. If people see that as weakness, they have forgotten about Christ. The truth is that Paul's action was "by God's power" (2 Corinthians 13:4).

The false apostles were not like that. Instead of having self-control for the benefit of others, they enslaved people, exploited them, took advantage of them, pushed themselves forward, and insulted the people with whom they "served" (2 Corinthians 11:20). It is not the person who can lash out at others quickly who is the person full of power, but rather the person who can maintain meekness and gentleness while others are demonstrating meanness and keeping grudges alive. Remember Paul started this section by saying, "By the meekness and gentleness of Christ." It would be easy for a person to look at a wild horse and say, "That's power," and then look at the same horse after he is tamed and conclude, "That's weakness," in comparison. That person would have made a serious error, for power under control is never weakness, but always strength. That was Christ on the cross, and that was Paul on his cross.

While some Corinthians wanted proof that Christ was speaking through Paul by his demonstration of power, they really had proof that Christ was speaking through him by Paul's demonstration of meekness and gentleness, which many of them interpreted as weakness. But Paul's meekness and gentleness did not mean weakness. He had given the wrongdoers enough time to grow up. And he would discipline the unrepentant ones on his third visit.

An Admonition (13:5-10)

Paul moved from issuing a warning to giving an admonition. While the Corinthians were asking for proof that Christ was speaking in Paul, Paul asked for them to give proof to themselves of their own faith. When Paul told them to "examine" themselves (2 Corinthians 13:5), he used the verb form of the same word that he used to describe the Corinthians' demand for "proof" from him (2 Corinthians 13:3). It is a word that refers to testing the genuineness of precious metals such as gold. Paul wanted them to apply some hard testing to themselves. While they wanted to know whether or not Christ was *speaking* through Paul, Paul wanted them to determine whether or not Christ was *living* in them. Paul wanted them to examine, test, and realize.

Paul did not believe that the Corinthians would fail the test, but wanted them to come firsthand to that realization. If they would come to realize that they were secure in Christ, then perhaps they would not be so quick to criticize and cut down someone else who was in Christ—namely Paul. It is much easier for a Christian to spot the genuineness of another Christian when he himself realizes his position in Christ. It is the Christian who is uncertain about himself who also demonstrates an uncertainty about others. That comes out then in criticism against others, in lack of patience with others, and in false charges against others. The very fact that some of the Corinthians had made it a life-style to do that with Paul and others is an indication of their low self-esteem and lack of security in Christ. Now, Paul wanted them to grow out of that.

From that kind of an examination comes a more determined commitment to do God's will in God's way. And it is for that reason that Paul prayed (2 Corinthians 13:7). But Paul did not desire that so people would think that he had had a successful ministry with them. He desired that for their good, not for his benefit. When the Corinthians put themselves to the test, some would discover that they were not living out what God wanted them to live. Those were the ones who had not yet repented. So while the self-examination would cause some to feel more secure, it would cause others to feel less secure. The ones who felt more secure could live more like Christ in not retaliating against Paul. Those who felt less secure could live more like Christ in repenting of their immorality. Out of that, all would do what was right. So when Paul said that Jesus did not want them to do anything wrong, that referred to the continuation of unrepented sins as well as the continuation of a critical spirit toward other Christians such as Paul.

If the Corinthians would change in toto before Paul would come, then Paul would not have to act sternly. And if that did happen, then some of the people would feel that Paul had failed, for some people think that a parent who does not come down hard on a wayward child has failed that child even though that child has straightened up. Paul was not going to be pushed into an improper reaction. He was going to live according to the truth that he knew and according to the truth that lived inside of him— and that truth was Jesus Christ, who gave him both what appeared to be weakness and who gave to him what was real power (2 Corinthians 13:8).

If the Corinthians would change without Paul's having to show his power, as the world understands power, Paul would be elated. That's what he meant when he said, "We are glad whenever we are weak but you are strong" (2 Corinthians 13:9). If he came to them in the weakness of a gentle spirit because they had become strong in their repentance and reaction, that would make Paul glad. Such weakness on his part as a result of strength on their part would be an answer to his prayer and a reason why he had written the way he had written (2 Corinthians 13:9, 10).

Paul had one concern for them, their "perfection" (2 Corinthians 13:9). The word for *perfection* indicates that Paul was hoping they would have mended what had been shattered or broken among them. It is from a Greek word that literally means to repair what is broken. It was used to put back together joints in a body that were disjointed. It is a word that describes the relationships with Christ and also with one another. It is indeed the result of a ministry of reconciliation that worked. And it is the result of the ministry of Paul that he invested "for building you up, not for tearing you down."

All Christian ministry should be evaluated by how it builds up people. For a Christian leader to use discipline selfishly just to show his power when the situation does not demand it, when it would destroy people, when it would not build up, when it would not manifest the power of Christ, is inappropriate for Christian ministry.

Closing Remarks (13:11-14)

In closing, Paul gave six quick commands, a greeting, and two blessings.

The Commands

1. "Rejoice." The NIV says "good-by," but the Greek is literally, "rejoice." It is out of a positive stance of joy that Christians can properly relate to God and to one another. Joy is a product of love and leads to peace. That's why the order of the fruit of the Spirit is, "love, joy, peace."

2. "Aim for perfection." The Greek word here is a word that describes the repairing of nets that had split. The idea is for the Corinthians to mend their broken relationships.

3. "Be comforted." The NIV says, "Listen to my appeal," but the literal Greek says, "Be comforted." He wanted the Corinthians to do for one another what God has done for us in our troubles. In a sense, he ended up giving the Corinthians the responsibility of doing what he discussed as he began this letter. God comforts us so that we can comfort others, he said (2 Corinthians 1:4). Remember the word *comfort* means to support someone. So Paul was asking for them to support one another, to stand by one another, to hold on to one another, and to encourage one another.

4. "Be of one mind." That's a Greek way to say, "Mend your differences."

5. "Live in peace." That means to live with the absence of alienation and retaliation. It means to manifest a life of reconciliation, not only to God, but also to each other.

6. "Greet one another with a holy kiss." Such a greeting expresses union and fellowship within the family. It was also an expression of mutual forgiveness and reconciliation. It was an outreach touch that showed acceptance. The "holy hug" or the firm handshake communicates the same in our western culture.

The Greeting

The greeting Paul shared was, "All the saints send their greetings" (2 Corinthians 13:13). This shows that Paul had not been bad-mouthing the Corinthians when he was with others. Other saints did not look down upon them nor write them out of the family of God. In fact, they encouraged Paul to be their proxy in greeting the Corinthians.

The Blessings

1. "And the God of love and peace will be with you" (2 Corinthians 13:14). That blessing came after Paul had talked about the Corinthians' taking on positive attitudes and activities with one another. The God of peace touches people who are positive. Paul outlined that in Philippians 4:7-9. And what he said there is re-stated here in a short-order form.

2. "May the grace of the Lord Jesus Christ, and the love of God, and the fellowship of the Holy Spirit be with you all" (2 Corinthians 13:14). That is the greatest benediction in the New Testament. Paul did not give it just to those who agreed with him, who had accepted him, who supported him, and who had repented. Paul gave it to "all" of them. Paul wanted the best from Jesus, from God, and from the Holy Spirit to touch their lives. That best was grace, love, and fellowship. *Grace* refers to any activity done for man's good. *Love* refers to that kind of love that sees one's need and moves to meet it without counting the cost. It is the kind of love that desires the success of another. And *fellowship* is the two-way participation where there is mutual sharing, respect, and help.

Paul wished the best from the finest to his family, the church. Perhaps it is this benediction that had controlled every motivation of Paul's dealings with the Corinthians. He wanted the grace of the Lord Jesus to be with them, so he shared His grace with them. He wanted the love of God to be with them, so he shared His love with them. He wanted the fellowship of the Holy Spirit to be with them, so he shared His fellowship with them despite all of the differences, difficulties, and problems that had existed.

Now we need to desire that benediction for others—and not just desire it, but also live it! For the grace of the Lord Jesus lives in us so that His grace can touch others through us. The love of God lives in us so God's love can touch others through us. The fellowship of the Holy Spirit lives in us so that His fellowship can minister to others through us. To do so is not just to wish that others receive the benefits of reconciliation, but it is also to offer ourselves as ministers of reconciliation.